NUHA AL-RADI

Baghdad Diaries

Born in Baghdad in 1941, Nuha al-Radi trained
at the Byam Shaw School of Art in London in
the early 1960s and later taught at the
American University of Beirut. A painter,
ceramist, and sculptor, her works have been
shown throughout the Arab world and in
Berlin, London, and Washington.

Baghdad Diaries

Baghdad Diaries

A Woman's Chronicle of

War and Exile

NUHA AL-RADI

Vintage Books
A Division of Random House, Inc.
New York

FIRST VINTAGE BOOKS EDITION, MAY 2003

Copyright © 1998, 2003 by Nuha al-Radi

All rights reserved under International and Pan-American Copyright Conventions. Published in the United States by Vintage Books, a division of Random House, Inc., New York, and simultaneously in Canada by Random House of Canada Limited, Toronto. Originally published in different form in Great Britain by Saqi Books, London, in 1998 and subsequently published in its present form by Saqi Books, London, in 2003.

The postscript originally appeared on the website for the Institute for War and Peace Reporting, www.iwpr.net.

Vintage and colophon are registered trademarks of Random House, Inc.

Portions of this book were originally published in *Granta* in 1992.

Cataloging-in-Publication Data is on file with the Library of Congress.

Vintage ISBN 1-4000-7525-4

www.vintagebooks.com

Printed in the United States of America
10 9 8 7 6 5 4 3 2 1

These diaries are dedicated to the people of Iraq and to all others who have suffered the crippling effects of war and sanctions.

My heartfelt thanks to my sister Selma who made the publication of these diaries possible, and to Toby Eady for his perseverance.

Contents

Baghdad Diaries

Prologue

I am to write, as usual, and as usual I say: I am not a writer. But I must update this diary to cover all the years since the published edition. Nothing really changes, only the years. As I look through my notebooks, I notice that some passages indicate the days and months and some have no date, but the year is always missing – a telling sign. I have titled the last chapter 'Identity' because I always seem to be chasing mine, via residence permits, visas or by constantly having to prove that I am an ordinary law-abiding person.

I now live in a third-floor flat in Beirut; through the windows I see buildings and a bit of sky, and one palm tree in the Saudi Embassy next door – a far cry from my Baghdad orchard with its 66 palms and 161 orange trees. When we first rented this flat in 1970 we used to have picnics on the nearby hillside; now you cannot see the hillside, let alone the sea, only a concrete jungle. But it is home.

In 1919, my father, an only child, was one of the first Iraqis to study in the USA (in Texas); his subject was agriculture. It wasn't so difficult being an Iraqi in those days. He went around the world with just a piece of paper from the British Consul, as Iraq was then under the British Mandate.

In 1947 he was made Ambassador, first to Iran and then India. To most Iraqis India meant snakes and tigers, but we loved India and stayed for nine years. With the revolution in

1958, my father was retired and returned to Baghdad. We each went abroad to study – my sister Sol (Selma) became an archaeologist and restorer, I became a ceramist (now painter) and my brother Dood (Abbad) an architect and planner. Sol is now married to Q (Qais), doctor and scientist, and Kiko (Rakkan) is her son from her first marriage. Dood is married to Shuhub and has a daughter and son.

My mother was one of four. Naira was her elder sister, better known as Needles: neat and coiffed even when sleeping. They had two brothers. Tariq became a gynaecologist in Britain, married and stayed there. The younger one, Mundhir Baig, was a good-looking charmer and wily lawyer.

Baghdad is built on both banks of the river Tigris. It winds through the city in a double 'S'. The northern and southern ends terminate in orchards, but by now the city has outgrown these limits.

When the war started in 1991, it seemed natural that family and friends should come and stay in my orchard. We felt safer being together; it was more economical and, yes, also fun. Our district, Suleikh, is at the north end of the city.

All the characters I speak about in this diary are relatives and friends.

Funduq al-Saada, or Hotel Paradiso

19 January 1991

On the eve of the war I went to the Rashid Hotel to pick up a letter that Bob Simpson[*] had brought from Charlie in Cyprus. He also sent me some seed packets of Italian vegetables, a tiny leak in the UN embargo. They will come in handy when we have water again. His room was full of hacks nattering away and waiting for the big moment. I told him very authoritatively that there would be no war.

'Wish I could believe you,' he said.

I'm not sure why I was so definite that there would be no war – my positive attitude had friends and family phoning me up for reassurance until the last day. Perhaps I simply couldn't believe that in this day and age leaders could be so childish and/or plain stupid as to think that war could solve any issue. I underestimated the destructive instincts of man and the agenda of the forces allied against us. Not that we are angels, after all we did the first wrong. But one cannot rectify one wrong by another of even bigger proportions. At least that's what I thought. After all, I witnessed at first hand three revolutions in Iraq, the Suez war in Egypt and some of the Lebanese civil war. Man's follies have no limits. In this instance, nobody wanted to communicate to allow for a compromise. As an Iraqi expression

---

[*]   BBC correspondent.

has it, one hand cannot clap alone. Obviously there is room for only one bully in this world.

The last six months of pre-war days were all the same, days sandwiched with nights; with the start of the war, days and nights became one long day. I don't have a 1991 calendar so I can't even tick the days off. It is all one. This is the third day of the war; it has taken me that long to realize that war has actually begun and I am not dreaming it. I have decided to write a diary, to keep some kind of record of what is happening to us. After all, this kind of thing doesn't happen every day.

Day 1

I woke up at 3 a.m. to the barrage of exploding bombs. I let out a huge groan that I can still hear. I couldn't believe that war had started. I went out on the balcony, the sky was lit up with the most extraordinary firework display – the noise was beyond description. My dog, Salvador Dalì, was chasing frantically round the two houses looking up at the sky and barking furiously. I couldn't get an answer from Ma and Needles'* phone so tried Suha who answered in a hushed voice from her shelter under the stairs, and told me to put out my lights. 'What for?' I asked. 'All the street lights are still on.' Suha, being a fastidious and efficient person, had taped all her windows and doors against nuclear fallout, and organized the windowless room under the stairs as her shelter and stashed it with provisions. I refused to take any such precautions, but Ma insisted on it and made a variety of designs on my windows, scrimping on the last ones as she ran out of tape.

Later on I ventured outside to put out the garage light. Salvador was very nervous. Shortly after that we lost all electricity, I needn't have bothered with putting the lights out. The phones followed suit and went dead. I think we are done for, a modern nation cannot fight without electricity and

---

*   The author's aunt.

communications. Thank heavens for our ration of Pakistani matches. Thinking of you Handy, glued to the television in Karachi – are you with us? Why are we being punished in this way?

With the first bomb, Ma and Needles' windows shattered, the ones facing the river. It's a good thing their shutters were down otherwise they could both have been badly hurt. One of poor Bingo's pups was killed in the garden by flying glass – our first war casualty. Bingo is the mother of Salvador Dalì. Myra, Ilham and the boys came in the morning, went and then returned to stay the night.

Day 2

Myra, Ilham and the boys went off to Khanaqin, they think they will be safer there. Amal and Munir, whose house is also on the river, lost all their windows the first night they moved in. Ma and Suha come and stay the nights, during the day they all go off to check on their own houses. Needles prefers to stay with Menth. My closest neighbour M.A.W. joins us for dinner; his wife is away in London.

Said came by and picked up Suha and me to have lunch with Taha. Said has a good supply of petrol but is not ready to give us any of it. We had kebab and beer; delicious. They were both quite unfazed by the situation and think that we are doing quite well. I can't think what they mean. No air raids *en route*. Salvador still barks wildly when the sirens go.

Today, all over Baghdad, government trucks threw bread to the thronging crowds.

Day 3

Suha and I spent the day merrily painting in my studio while the war was going on full blast outside. I wonder where this detachment comes from, whilst others are gnashing their teeth with fear. This afternoon we saw a SAM missile explode in the sky. I also caught Mundher Baig riding around on his grandson's tricycle, scrunched up with his legs under his chin, pedalling round and round in his driveway. He said he was enjoying himself. He misses his grandchildren and is convinced that he will not see them again.

At night we had a fire in the orchard. At first we thought it was war damage but in fact it was Fulayih's fault. He had been burning some dry wood near the dead core of a palm tree, trying to turn it into coal. We used up all our water, Dood's house and mine combined, plus the fire extinguisher from the car to put out this fire. Now we have no water, and Fulayih has no coal.

Day 4
Woke up to an air raid at 5 a.m. Went to Zaid's house to leave a message and saw his two old aunts, each probably 110 years old; one was bent double over the stove while the other never stopped chattering beside her. Because of the constant air raids they are afraid to go upstairs to their bedrooms so they sleep in their clothes on couches in the sitting room, missing their familiar mattresses and pillows. They seem oblivious to the enormity of what's happening around them, concentrating only on the immediate things, so old and frail yet so alive and entertaining. Their phone still works so I tried to call Assia and Suha whose house is right across the river from the Dora refinery. A huge black sky covers that part of Baghdad. It must be horrific living there. No one answered the telephone.

Mundher Baig started a generator for their house on precious and scarce petrol. Ten of us just stood around gaping in wonder at this machine and the noise it made. Only four days have passed since the start of the war and already any machinery and mod cons seem to be totally alien, like something from Mars.

Suha is experimenting with making *basturma** from the meat in her freezer. Our freezers are beginning to defrost, so it's a good thing that it's so cold.

Salvador continues to attack M.A.W., who aggravates him by brandishing his walking stick at him; we now have to escort him in and out of the orchard. At dinner M.A.W.'s stomach growled and Ma thought it was an air raid. Cooked potatoes in the fireplace, trying to save on gas. M.A.W. said one could taste the potato in the smoke, admittedly they were charred. The sky is a wondrous sight at night, every star clearly shining amidst the fireworks and the continuous noise of explosions. I hope Sol and Dood are not too worried about us. They should know that we are survivors.

Made a dynamic punch tonight with Aquavit, vodka and fresh orange juice. We ate fish and rice.

Day 5

Munir gave me a calendar today. It's 21 January. My painting of Mundher Baig and family is nearly finished. Got my bicycle fixed. It's a brand new one, never been used, and we had been trying for days to inflate the tyres. They both turned out to have punctures. I told the guy who was mending it that it was new. 'They always come like this,' he said. Does someone actually puncture them before they leave the factory? It's an Iraqi bike, imaginatively called Baghdad. It's a good thing they didn't call it Ishtar; her name already dignifies fridges, freezers, soap, matches, heaters and hotels. You name it, it's called Ishtar. That proud goddess of war would not have liked her name being associated with such lowly things. Imagination is not our strongest point when it comes to naming things.

We are now all going to the loo in the orchard, fertilizing it and saving ourselves some water which no longer flows out of the taps. Janette comes by every day. She says everyone has

---

*   Cured sausages.

gone off to the countryside because it's the best place to be during a war. Then she said, 'But your house is like being in the country anyway, and that's the best place to be in. Lucky you.' She's so right. None of us is budging from this orchard paradise, which it truly is. She is looking around for a bedfellow today, quite crazed. I said it wasn't uppermost in my mind right now.

Basil came by and I told him to put his mind to work on basic agriculture. Now that we are back in the Dark Ages, we have to figure out a way to haul up water from the river. He is cooking up all the foodstuff he had in his freezer and feeding it to his cats. His wife and daughters can't be bothered.

Apparently people have taken off for the countryside with their freezers loaded on their pick-up trucks. They eat their way through the food as it defrosts – barbecues in the country. Quite mad. Only we would escape from a war carrying freezers full of goodies. Iraqis have been hoarders for centuries. It's a national habit. Since one never knows when anything will be available on the market, one buys when one sees, and in great quantities. Most people automatically queue up when they see a line forming, not caring what's at the other end; boot polish, soap, tomatoes or a useless gadget. Needles says she is running out of chickens when she has twenty left in the freezer.

Day 6

Got up for the regular 5 a.m. air raid. It finished an hour later. We go and queue for petrol – our ration: 20 litres. Amal, who never remembers to wear her glasses, backed into a wall.

The entire country has collapsed and disintegrated in a few days. They say that outside Baghdad everything appears to be normal. I wonder how long we can survive this kind of bombardment. This afternoon Muwafaq and Ala' brought a hysterical, crying Hind. They wanted to come and stay here. Hind screamed and cried all the time. She insists on dragging everyone down to their cellar every air raid, now she wants to drag the entire household (grandmother, mother, brother, fiancé and herself) to Khanaqin. No one wanted to go there; the alternative was to come here. Poor Maarib, who is not well and has trouble with her eyes, does not want to be parted from her own bathroom. In normal times she takes about five baths a day and puts cream all over her body after each one. I go to their car. Hind is still crying. I am very stern with her – rules of the house are no crying, no guns, no smoking. She continues to howl, saying, 'I'm scared, I don't want to die.' No stopping her waterworks, they leave undecided.

Today is the sixth day. I hope we get water tomorrow.

Day 7

The worst has happened – beer without ice. Cleaned out the freezer and removed a ton of different kinds of bread. All I ever had in my freezer was bread, ice and bones for Salvador. Asma had so much chicken in hers that she gave some away and grilled the rest. Now Nofa goes around chewing on chicken rather than her usual chocolate bars. She is keeping those for harder times, she says.

Following Suha's recipe for *basturma*, Ma began making her own. None of us has ever made *basturma* before and we thought that it would be a good way to preserve our meat. We minced raw meat and mixed it with a lot of different spices and salt, and then stuffed the mixture into nylon stockings (in lieu of animal intestines, which were not available). Suha's hand mincer was resurrected and put to use. We are using Dood's house as our fridge – all that marble, what a come-down. My bread covers all the tables and the *basturmas* hang above.

We have to eat an enormous amount of food so as not to throw it away. This means we shit so much more – all is done in the garden. If we use the bathroom, we fear that the sewage will back up on us – I have only now discovered that electricity moves it. One takes so much for granted. Wonder whether the Allies thought of such things when they were planning the bombing. I don't think we will be seeing electricity for a long time to come.

Started burning the rubbish today and clearing the orchard of dead matter. Amal was helping, wearing her usual high heels even for collecting brambles.

Rumour had it that we were going to have a difficult night ahead. This is the seventh night, maybe Bush thinks he is God too. But it clouded over, so maybe God was on our side tonight. Now there are three gods. Who will win?

We got some water today but the pressure was too weak to get it up to the tank on the roof. Never mind. I'm not complaining. At least we got to fill up all the buckets. All our drinking water must be boiled now.

I finished Mundher's painting so we had a little party to celebrate its unveiling. Everyone was impressed and thought I deserved a prize. We opened a bottle of champagne and ate *meloukhia** and a million other things. I wish that our stock of food would finish so that we could eat a little less. M.A.W.'s sister and brother-in-law fled their house in Fahama and came to live with him. Now there are two more for dinner. She left dressed in a green suit, which is all she possesses now. They huddle together for security. She is sweet but hardly says a word. He never stops talking and is as deaf as a post. He is probably the last surviving communist in this country. In his youth he was well known for singing old Iraqi songs, so he entertained us and lulled us all to sleep with his nice voice – sleeping heads lolling in different directions.

Day 8

Silence reigns. It's six in the morning, and no air raid. I ate so much last night that I couldn't go to sleep. Depression has hit me with the realization that the whole world hates us and is really glad to ruin us. It's not a comforting thought. It's an

---

*   A type of stew, made with a strongly flavoured green vegetable.

unfair world. Other countries do wrong. Look at what Russia did in Afghanistan, or Turkey's invasion of Cyprus, or Israel taking over Palestine and Lebanon. Nobody bombed them senseless the way we are being bombarded now. They were not even punished. Iraq has had many high and low peaks in its long history, we have certainly become notorious. This will be neither the first nor the last time. 'Too much history,' as Sol always says. At least Baghdad is now on the map. I will no longer have to explain where I come from.

I had these two dreams before the start of the war: the Americans in battle fatigues jogging down Haifa Street and lining up in the alleyways, kissing each other. They were led by a girl dressed in red who was running very fast. Then suddenly the scene switched and I was coming out of the house and everything was dry as dust, just earth, and I was all alone. I said to myself, 'I will build and plant it so that it will be the most beautiful garden.' Later, what bothered me about this dream was the loneliness of it. Am I going to be the only survivor?

Day 9

Funny thing, since the war started I have not been able to read a word, not even a thriller. Instead I'm writing this diary, not something I normally do. Ma, who usually never stops knitting, can't knit. Instead, Suha and Amal, who have no talent in that direction, have started to knit. Fastidious Asam, who normally changes her clothes twice a day, now does so every other day. She also sleeps in them. She hid all the scissors in her house in case someone attacks her with them. I asked what about the knives? A shrug of the shoulders was all I got in response. She also placed her jewellery in boxes that were heavily wrapped in plastic bags and buried them in the garden, hoping that she will remember the exact spot.

People's reactions to the strains of the situation are funny and strange. Last night I took out a red dress to wear and went to have my wash with my allotted kettle's worth of water. I came out of the bathroom and couldn't find my dress anywhere. I wore something else, saying I would look for it in the morning. I still cannot find it; what did I do with it?

Today, Abla Jalila, sitting upright in true Ottoman manner, sirens wailing outside, says to me, 'Why don't we take the Taurus Express train and go to Istanbul?'

I said, 'What makes you think the trains are running? Nothing else is.' Admittedly, she is becoming a little deaf and since she left her house to stay with Talal seems even more distracted than usual. Her house is in the firing line, fairly close to Henry's. I passed by him to convince him to come and join us; he opened the door ashen-faced, but refused to move out of his house. His real fear is being caught in a bombing raid with his pants down. He has to think carefully every time he goes to the loo.

I'm trying to get M.A.W. to use his time constructively. I gave him my wall clock to repair. He complained endlessly, then started to fiddle with it and got it to work. He's excellent at mending things, having an endless supply of patience for machines but almost none for life and people.

Water situation is becoming bad. People have taken to doing their washing in the river, which is very fast flowing. Its high and steep banks don't help.

They captured an island in the Gulf that only appears at low tide. We didn't even know its name.

Day 10

I say 'Read my Lips', today is the tenth day of the war and we are still here. Where is your three to ten days swift and clean kill? Mind you, we're ruined. I don't think I could set foot in the West again. If someone like myself who is Western educated feels this way, then what about the rest of the country? Maybe I'll just go to India. I don't know if it's because we grew up there that I have such a close affinity to that country, or because they have a high tolerance level and will not shun us Iraqis.

Suha mended her bike today. Hers was also new and punctured. We rode out together and caused a sensation in the streets. All very friendly. One guy also on a bike sidles by us and says, 'Actually, I have a Mercedes at home.'

'Are we in Paris?' says another.

One sour man says, 'We don't have girls who ride bikes!' We yelled at him, 'More fool you,' and pedalled away. Nofa says I look like ET because I'm wrapped in a hundred scarves and they fly behind me. More like a witch, I'd say.

Tomorrow I'll be fifty years old. I feel very depressed. We're in such a mess and it's all so sad. So many people have to die, and for what?

M.A.W. says we can get electricity in one minute if we attach ourselves to Turkey or Jordan because we have a connected circuit. Yesterday we heard we may be getting it from Iran. What can they connect it to if they have bombed the stations?

Everyone talks endlessly about food. While eating lunch, it's what we're having for dinner. People's freezers are beginning to empty. One goes visiting and is given a defrosting chicken and green beans to take home. We cooked up all the meat we had in our various houses. The *basturmas* that we had hung up in Dood's house are starting to stink – the whole house has begun to reek.

Hala says she will give me a bucket of water as my birthday present.

Day 11

I had great hopes for my birthday but in fact stayed sad and depressed. Me and Mozart share the same day. Lots of people were invited. They all came and more. Drinks flowed in buckets. Someone peed on my bathroom floor. I'm sure it was that horrid Mazin who came uninvited. Fuzzle stayed the night.

She says to Yasoub, 'Take me out to pee,' and they went out into the garden arm in arm, so romantically after all these years of marriage. Lovely big moon out. Fuzzle entertained us with stories about her air-raid shelter. She goes there every night with Mary, her Indian maid, from six in the evening 'til seven the next morning, when they unlock the doors. There are three tiers, hierarchical order with the biggies being at the lowest level. At each level there are three tiers of bunks, bodies on top of bodies. She gets very nervous when the bombing starts. Being diabetic, her blood count shoots up and she gets scared and starts shaking. We must all have the hides of rhinos here in this house. No one seems afraid. It was a particularly bad night and we had to take her mind off the noisy bombing outside – she was used to the quiet of the shelter with only the soldiers singing out to Mary, Mary...

Day 12
We got water today from the garden tap – pressure is too low for the water to reach the kitchen taps. Drew endless buckets of water up to the tank on the roof. I filled them up and Munir pulled them up with a rope, eighty buckets in all. Very hard work, and I got sopping wet in the process. Back to Stone Age basics.

Another freezing day with the usual air raids.

Day 13
I'm typing by candlelight and can see very little, maybe this won't be readable tomorrow. Ma and Suha went to the *souq* today to buy more lanterns and an air raid started. No one bothered to move or go home, everyone carried on their business as usual. In fact, there was such a crush of people that Ma and Suha managed to lose each other. Maybe Iraqis have no fear. They were bombing the bridge at Southgate. The shock caused all the doors of the buildings in the vicinity to blow open. All the windows went, broken glass everywhere – a real

mess. Amal's shop, which is right beside the bridge, also got blown. Now both her house and her shop are damaged. She never complains and is very stoic. Mundher Baig went to check on our building. He just stood there and cried, thinking about Grandpa and what he would have thought of all this.

Since it was Suhub's birthday, we all met at their house for lunch. Driving across the Adhamiya Bridge, we could see black columns of smoke rising in all directions. It seems they are burning a lot of tyres to confuse the enemy. Some confusion. Samih said that an unexploded rocket had fallen in the garden of the Rashid Hotel. There was a mad scrabble for bits as mementoes before the security forces closed access to it. Mundher Baig came to the party from seeing the destruction in Southgate. He was very upset and kept repeating again and again to Ma, 'Our country has gone. What do you think will happen now?' Ma consoled him in her usual philosophical way by telling him that as it was ruined it would be rebuilt. 'I'll not see it,' he said.

Are we in for a nuclear war? I must say I don't feel there is a risk of death, at least for myself. I know that I'm going to survive this somehow. Twenty-seven thousand air raids on us so far. Is the world mad? Do they not realize what they're doing? I think Bush is a criminal. This country is totally ruined. Who gives the Americans the licence to bomb at will? I could understand Kuwait doing this to us, but not the whole world. Why do they hate us so much?

This peasant's life that we now lead is very hard; work never stops. I am usually the first person up. I come down, having refused to leave my upstairs bedroom. Some are still snoring. Suha leaves and goes to her house to do her ablutions. She doesn't like our primitive toilet arrangements. Each of us has different chores to do. I collect firewood, clean the grate and make up the fire for the evening. I clean and sweep up a bit around the kitchen where all meals take place, and boil the water for coffee. Food is usually cooked by Suha and Amal, and sometimes by Ma though her main responsibility is making bread and cakes. Mine is making the soups and salads. I pick and clean all the salad materials – lettuce, radish, celery, rocket, parsley and green coriander all grow in the orchard. I have four buckets of water for washing these greens; the dirty water is never wasted. It is then used for watering the garden or trees. Lunch is usually a simple snack. Dinner is early – between seven and eight – our one real meal of the day. Sometimes it's accompanied by bombing; other times not.

I have learned to do a lot of things in the dark but none of us has learned to sleep early. In fact, we sleep very little, adrenalin keeps us going. The snoring at night can be categorized into different types. Ma snores in small puffs, Amal's is like a steam engine. The other night Munir dreamed that he was living *Star Wars* very vividly, only to wake up with a start and realize that it was the harmony of different snores. He promptly went back to sleep again.

Salvador has got a new and horrid girlfriend. He bit Said yesterday. He is not a strokable dog.

Day 14
Mundher Baig died in his sleep early this morning. The war now seems very far away. Life is too immediate. We listen to the news, sirens, rockets, and bombs come and go. We are unmoved, it might as well be taking place on another planet. It's true that he had a bad heart and yesterday he ran up nine floors to check the damage to our building. But he really died of sorrow. He could not comprehend why the world wanted to destroy us – us the people, us the city, and all that we had built up during the last fifty years. He kept asking Ma yesterday, 'Why are they doing this to us?' It's strange, but I knew all during the time that I was painting his portrait that the painting would never hang normally in their house. To take this dread feeling away, I hurried and finished it and had the unveiling in

my house even before the paint was dry. Sure enough, it is still here, drying. He was not made for dying, so lively and full of energy, good for laughter and for fights. He helped everybody. We are going to miss him a lot, a lot.

We each had to take a section of Baghdad and drive around to inform friends and relatives of the funeral. I went to Mansur,* crossing the Adhamiya Bridge during a full-scale air raid. Normally we cross the river only after the planes have gone away in case the bridge gets hit while one is driving across it. This time I didn't bother to wait. Sirens were going off, rockets and bombs were falling. I was unmoved.

Lubna says she saw a plane fall in Karrada. Later it turned out to be a Cruise missile.

I finally managed to send notes to Dood and Sol. Poor guys, they must be so worried. The isolation we feel is unimaginable.

Day 15

Amal went to pick some firewood from near the garage area and came back with one of Salvador's trophies, an old yellow shoe that he had stashed in the firewood. It had been a present from my Kurdish guard and gardener, Tawfiq, who had bought a job lot of shoes from the Kadhum, including this single, yellow shoe. Poor guy, he was called up in December to join the army. I wonder where he is now? How could Amal have mistaken an old shoe for a piece of firewood? Her eyes must be worse than one thought, a real hazard on the road. Good thing there's little driving to do.

All the water that Munir and I hauled up to the roof tank yesterday leaked into the downstairs bathroom. A real tragedy. This loo is jinxed. I have lived here for three years and have had to change it twice already. This new loo has been fixed at least five times and the handle has been changed twice, and yet it still leaks. Life is very hard.

---

*   New wealthy, middle-class area of Baghdad.

Went and helped Amal clean up her shop, mostly a mess of broken glass. Her brother came with big sheets of plywood and boarded up the place. Saw the Jumhuriya Bridge from there, nice neat holes with a lot of metal hanging down underneath. Found a bit of shrapnel by the river. The bridge was packed with people gaping at the holes. A siren sounded but nobody budged.

Day 16

The women are gathered in Asma's house for Mundher Baig's '*aza*.* Ma and Needles' house is being used for the men's *fatiha*,** and I have been put in charge of that. Quite unconventional as I keep charging in and chatting to various bods. On the whole I am behaving myself. Word is getting around Baghdad that Mundher Baig died and people are coming from all over, using up their hoarded petrol, crying and bewailing his loss. All of them told me that he had come round to visit them recently. Apparently during his last week he had been going round Baghdad by bus, checking up on all of his friends, and saying goodbye to them. He must have sensed his coming death.

We may be getting electricity from Qasr Shireen in Iran, but it's all rumours. Nobody knows anything. There's a total lack of local information. Baghdad Radio broadcasts for a few hours a day, giving us battle information ... how many planes we brought down, what the enemy is doing to us and how we are fighting back. Propaganda galore to keep up our spirits. Nobody pays much attention. We listen to Radio Monte Carlo at eight; at night there's the BBC or Voice of America; Radio Austria, I have discovered, is quite sympathetic and actually remembers that there are people living here.

---

*   Mourning ceremony.

**   Part of the mourning ceremony during which the opening *sura* of the Qur'an (the *fatiha*) is recited.

Everyone here is living a village life in their own immediate section of the town. Little petrol, only enough for emergencies, and the few buses that run are overcrowded. Any contact between different parts of Baghdad is difficult and sometimes impossible. Poor soldiers at the front. Their situation must be a million times worse than ours.

Salvador's new girlfriend crawls in through holes in the orchard fence. I keep plugging them up but they find new entry points. I had to get up and shoo them away at five this morning. They were making such a racket. Howling dogs combined with the barrage in the sky was simply too much to bear. The only good thing about this dog is that she keeps Salvador busy and exhausts him enough so that we can go to the loo in peace. Otherwise he playfully attacks and terrorizes anyone squatting behind a tree. Amal has it the worst. He grabs at her trousers and tries to pull them off. He thinks it's a wonderful game. Now she's taken to giving him a bone every time she has to go to the loo. That occupies his attention.

Day 17
An awful night. Rocketing non-stop and the biggest and loudest explosion ever. It was apparently heard all over Baghdad but no one seems to know where it was. Not atomic anyway. We are still alive. I can understand the Kuwaitis hating us but what did we do to you, George Bush, that you should hate us with such venom? One can hear it in your voice. Is it because we stood up to the USA and said no?

Tonight we shall have music. Amal has an old crank-up Victrola gramophone and M.A.W., who never throws anything away, has a lot of 78 rpm records that we can now play on it. Who could have conceived of such a day when the rest of the world has CDs?

Wadad came by today and showed us how to make a candle using a bottle filled with kerosene and a wick. One seals the bottle neck with a mash of dates, leaving only a small section of the wick sticking out – a long wick produces columns of smoke. At least we can produce something. Normal candles leave much to be desired. They splutter, they drip, they grow enormous wicks and spew forth a lot of black smoke – in fact, they leave a terrible mess everywhere. This bottle candle lasts for ages, it's safer and less messy. I thought it much like a Molotov cocktail but Wadad informed me that a Molotov is made with petrol whereas this is filled with kerosene.

This morning there was a huge number of dead flies on the floor. I wonder if the big explosion shocked them to death?

I had a great fight with Salvador. He was cavorting with his white fluffy floozie in one of my flower beds. They have an entire orchard to gad about in. Why pick on my flower beds? I may have to kill all these wild dogs. They could be carrying all sorts of diseases. I don't know what all these lady dogs see in Salvador. He doesn't seem to be that interested in them. His sexual attentions are centred on a favourite cushion.

We are a multitude of women in the Suleikh.* No men. Now M.A.W. says he wants to leave too. He was touched when we asked him not to. Life would certainly be duller without him.

Day 18
Last night M.A.W. said, 'Wars must be continuous. I have now got so used to eating charred food that when we finish this war we must start another.' We are saving gas by cooking and heating food in the fireplace, which seems to be smoking. Maybe something is wrong with the chimney. We are baking our own bread. The favourite way is to place the unleavened dough flat on fine wire mesh, like pitta bread, and bake it on an Aladdin stove. These old kerosene stoves have proven their worth. They are the best heaters and now the best bread-makers. No Iraqi home is without one. People discovered that

---

*　　Long-established, wealthy, middle-class area of Baghdad.

M.A.W. has a huge roll of wire mesh and started to queue up for their share. He has it all cut up and grudgingly doles it out.

Every night I dream of totally unreal things. Last night it was people standing outside third-floor windows, just naturally hanging around in mid-air and having a conversation, just like a cocktail party.

The birds have taken the worst beating of all. They have sensitive souls which cannot take all this hideous noise and vibration. All the caged love-birds have died from the shock of the blasts, while birds in the wild fly upside down and do crazy somersaults. Hundreds, if not thousands, have died in the orchard. Lonely survivors fly about in a distracted fashion.

The sky is now covered with black clouds. We are fighting and confusing the enemy with our usual burning tyres. Meanwhile they use computer technology to destroy us. An astronaut on a Russian satellite said he saw huge black clouds and many fires burning across the region.

Salvador has gotten more used to the noise of the explosions, but a very loud bang still sends him chasing about distractedly. Dogs seem to sense an air raid before it begins. They tense up and start barking before we can hear anything. I wonder why they don't use them instead of radar? Wild dogs pile up against Salvador for comfort during bad air raids. He has us for his security; they have him. Some of them actually cry with fear, making the most awful and pathetic sounds.

We've now been without water for one week. My hands and nails are disgusting. Everyone has a sooty face. No one bothers to look in the mirror any more. Needles is the only one who still looks neat and clean. Raad says that in Jadiriyah they have no more day; the sky is permanently black from the smoke of the Dora refinery as it burns. It has been burning from the first day of the war. Poor Suha and Assia; how are they surviving?

Day 19

Two rockets fell in the Masbah. One on Salwan and Uns's garden smashed through their outside wall and into part of the garage. They were all in the sitting room at the time – they are OK, if somewhat shaken. Suha and Assia, who live next door, were apparently filmed by CNN, ranting and raving about the war. The second rocket fell on a house right in front of Peggy and Naji's and smashed every window in theirs. Miraculously, only Naji was cut by a piece of flying glass. Four days before the rocket fell on that house, the people who had temporarily rented it (after fleeing from Kuwait) had moved to a hotel because it had no water. Another miracle.

There is nothing nice about war. The one thing that no one bet on was that Baghdad was going to be bombed and hit like this. They were supposed to be freeing Kuwait. Maybe they need a map? No one will hear from us for years, that is if we come out of this in one piece and alive.

Mundher Baig dead. I really can't believe it.

Lubna came by today. Robbers stole their generator and Mahmood's petrol which he had buried in the garden. They must have been keeping a close watch. Stealing has become the latest fashion. Everything has to be kept under lock and key. Generators go for thousands, bicycles too. Cigarettes are worth a fortune, and kerosene lamps are valued like gold. Shopkeepers who live near their stores stay open, but most goods are sold off crate tops on the sidewalks, odd bods selling wicks, batteries, matches – anything that is available. The other day a house was robbed and when the owners reported it to the police they said, 'We have no petrol to make a special visit. It will have to wait 'til we go on a patrol in that area.'

Day 20

It has now been three weeks: 44,000 air raids. I have another leak in the waterworks. I will have to check the whole house.

Bush says, we make war to have peace. Such nonsense. What a destructive peace this is. A new world order? I call it disorder.

Day 21

One week since Mundher Baig died. My hands are now so calloused they look like farmers' hands. Ma says she feels like Scarlett O'Hara in *Gone With the Wind* ... except that we are far from starving.

They have started hitting the bridges again. Jumhuriya Bridge is now apparently in three pieces. Countless industries, textile factories, flour mills and cement plants are being hit. What do they mean when they say they are only hitting military targets? These are not military installations. As for 'our aim never goes wrong' . . . who will save us from these big bullies? Maybe they want to destroy us so they can produce more jobs for their people in the West! Reconstruction and new military supplies could keep them going economically for years.

Thamir's chickens have stopped producing eggs. They used to lay twenty-five eggs a day, then two, and now none. On the other hand, Pat's chickens have never laid so many eggs.

Last night I dreamed I was carrying a tree. It grew little bread buns on it which I offered around. It had no roots or they were in the air, I'm not sure which. Anyway, I was happily walking around with it. Nice. A miracle tree?

Day 22

There is a sameness about the days now.

I saw the Jumhuriya Bridge today. It's very sad to see a bombed bridge. A murderous action, for it destroys a link. Everyone is very strangely affected by the sight of a bombed bridge. They cram along the sides, peering down into the craters and holes, looking very sad and crying.

Meanwhile children have never had it so good. They play on the streets with no fear of cars. They ride their bikes and enjoy themselves. I am called Bicycletta by all the kids in the streets. They wave and ask me how I am when I pass by. I say fine, or not, depending on my mood. Everyone now knows their neighbours, children and grown-ups alike. The Suleikh is like one big village. In fact, the city of Baghdad has turned into pockets of little villages.

I saw Riadh and Rabab on the street and went in for a coffee to their house. Rabab was the only person who was convinced that there would be a war. She proudly switched on the light in the kitchen; their refrigerator was working too – all on one generator rigged by Riadh, whose practical talents now show their value. Rabab told me that everyone should have a Riadh in the house. His hobby has always been mending old cars. He recently bought a rare old French car which he is slowly working on. His garage is full of wrecks in various stages of repair. They have asked me to come and watch television with them in the evening; they get Iranian television. Lots of women in chadors. Sometimes, even Iraqi television comes on for about half an hour. I hope to make it one evening but it will be difficult since I am the fire- and lamp-lighter for all my house guests.

Day 23
Went to Dhafir and Mutaza to teach them how to make kerosene candles. She broke her tooth yesterday. They called their dentist friend who lives nearby and he told them he had no petrol to run his generator. So they drew about five litres of petrol from their car and went off to the clinic with it. Dhafir decided to take advantage of the situation and redid a filling. Ma said, 'I wish you had told me too.'

The equivalent of five Hiroshimas have already been dropped on us. We were all restless last night and could not sleep because there were no air raids. At midnight we got an air raid, and everyone promptly went to bed. It's odd, but the same thing used to happen to us in Beirut. We went to sleep quite happily to the sound of shelling but woke up the minute the cacophony stopped.

Days 24 and 25
I tell you, there is this sameness. Even war becomes a routine.

Day 26
'It's Monday morning,' says the Voice of America. What's the difference? We had a bad night, the worst yet. The minute the all-clear sounded we went to check up on friends and relatives. We have developed a routine route. We piled into Yahya's car. This time he sacrificed his precious petrol which he had been saving up for visiting his fiancée who lives at the other end of town, in Mansur. We first stopped by Asam's house where everyone was huddled by the entrance – during air raids it is the most protected place. An assorted mixture of friends and family usually stay the night there, keeping company. She has tall, double-storeyed, stained-glass windows which reflect the war sky as through a kaleidoscope – very dramatic. It's amazing they are still in one piece. We next went and checked on Muhammad at Ma and Needles' house. It was a coal-black night, so dark that we could hardly make out the river; even the stars were hiding tonight. Muhammad slept through the whole thing; even the dogs were hushed in that house. Our last stop was Adiba's house. She opened the door for us crying and screaming in a hysterical fashion, and repeating over and over again, 'Please God either take my life or that of the bridge.' She looked a wonderful sight, wearing a jumble of bright colours in her Kurdish way. The house is very close to the Adhamiya Bridge which they have been trying to knock out for two days now. The noise and the vibrations have been unbearable. Instead of hitting that bridge they got a whole group of houses. Wonder why they're missing their target. Tomorrow we'll know what they have hit or missed.

The Martyrs' Bridge and the Suspension Bridge have been hit. I feel very bitter towards the West.

Day 27

Apparently the racket that we heard yesterday was the sound of the B-52 bombers. They sounded horrific. Menth got a bullet through the front windshield of his parked car.

I read this somewhere the other day: 'Every scientist has intuitions and they scare the hell out of him 'til he can test them.' Is that true or false, Doc?

Fat cats everywhere. Fat cats sleeping, or sitting in doorways; fat cats walking and crossing the streets with no fear of being run over. They of all creatures seem to be totally unmoved by what is happening around them. They have been eating to bursting point on all the leftovers from the thawing freezers. Meat and chicken have been passed around like nuts – but the end is in sight. Salvador will have to get used to being a vegetarian quite soon. Kiko* would be happy!

Talking about freezers, Sheikha came back yesterday to her house. She had spent the first three weeks at her daughter's house and only came back at the behest of her neighbours, who could not stand the smell coming out of her house. She put on a face mask and emptied her giant freezer. Right on top, floating on a sea of stagnant scummy water, was an entire sheep, and bobbing around it were twenty-four chickens and sundry legs of lamb in various states of decay. Two dozen *kubbas*,** sixty-eight rice patties, plus plastic bags full of stuffed vegetables, beans and peas, all of which had been frozen and put away for the hard times to come. Three whole fishes, hunks of beef, kilos of mince, loaves of bread, cakes and pastries – all had to be thrown out, adding to the diet of the bloated street animals who have never had it so good. By the way, this description of the contents

---

*   The author's nephew.
**   Stuffed meatballs.

of Sheikha's freezer could just as easily apply to every well-to-do household in Baghdad before the start of the war. Everyone was preparing and hoarding foodstuffs in their freezers, never imagining that they would bomb us out of electricity. Now the big question is whether to keep the freezer and fridge doors open or closed. If they stay open the rubber seals will dry out, and if closed they smell.

Most people have run out of petrol, and it doesn't appear likely that we will be getting any more in the near future. So it's either pedalling on the bike, walking, or going by bus. Buses are still running but they are packed. A few families took precautions and hoarded petrol in tanks in their gardens – there have been many accidents. Munir U. built large tanks in Najul's garden but didn't check them for leaks. Now he says the petrol has all gone – perhaps he sold it to Basil for a huge sum of money. Petrol is so scarce that some dealers mix it with water. One has to buy it from a reliable source and check its colour. Pinky-mauve is the best.

Some are thinking about going to shelters for the night. Suha and I offered to go and check ours out, although I would never go and spend the night there. The Suleikh shelter is inside Baghdad College, the old Jesuit school for boys, in the grounds of what used to be a monastery and vineyard in the tenth century – the monks were famous for their wine. Wish it was wine instead of war now. The shelter is a big, plain, windowless block. They are the same design all over Baghdad, built by the Swedes. A claustrophobic nightmare. Inside there was low-voltage electricity, not even enough to read by. Very high ceilings. 'You can register your name,' said the guard at the door, 'and come or not come. But if you do want to come, you must be here by six. That's when the doors shut.' The doors look like massive metal walls.

My next-door neighbour and her three daughters have been going there for the last couple of nights. Her husband is stuck in

Tunis and she says her daughters are less nervous and sleep better there without the noise – but it's not quite paradise, she added.

I came back late from Asam's house, where I had been informing them about the shelters, to find my driveway full of cars. The house had been invaded by ten more human beings between the ages of five and eighty. Apparently, today's broadcast said that all radio stations were going to be bombed. They had all been staying together in one house near a radio station. Now they want to stay here – they couldn't think of anywhere else to go. I have taken to calling us Hotel Paradiso. Every inch of the house is now occupied, people playing cards, others listening to the radio and still others boozing away. I can't stand it for too long. I will have to see what can be arranged tomorrow – maybe divide them all up between this house and Dood's.

Day 28

I am continuously amazed by the good quality of the construction of our houses. Everything shakes and rattles, and yet they are still intact and in one piece. Last night was another horror, maybe the worst yet. I felt each and every thermostone move in the house. The whole of Baghdad shook. They were trying to get at the bridge again. No one slept much. We went and checked on Adiba again. She is not certain why her house is still standing. She's locked up with that horror of a husband and the bombing. She definitely has the worst of all worlds. Why couldn't he have died instead of Mundher Baig? Not many would mourn his death, mean old devil that he is. That's not a very nice thing to say, but I can't help it.

Why do they keep bombing the same things again and again? Every one of these bloody rockets costs a quarter of a million dollars or more. Instead of feeding the hungry of the world, billions are spent on manufacturing more and more sophisticated weapons of destruction. Killing is the new world order.

Muayad and Donny came to visit. Archaeological sites have also been hit. A few arches have fallen in Hatra, Ctesiphon has new cracks, and the doors of the Mustansiriya exploded open. There is also some damage to the museum from flying shrapnel and debris from the bombing of the telephone exchange across the street. Muayad wonders about the state of other sites but does not have the petrol to go and check them. Where would one start in this country anyway? He is especially worried about the Samarra minaret since the factories and houses nearby (with everyone in them) have been virtually flattened. They spend their time checking up on the historic buildings around Baghdad, and boarding up their broken windows. Donny is photographing all the damage as evidence for the future. Robbers instantly descend on a building that gets hit or whose windows are smashed. The two make a wonderful sight – stomachs expanding forward unchecked. Nobody pays attention any more to the old law of weight control that required all civil servants to be checked every six months. Each height had its weight limit, and if it was exceeded the person was demoted. The ambitious lost weight, the pleasure-loving or couldn't-care-less got demoted or resigned. The Iraqi figure definitely improved under this law.

Salvador has a new girlfriend, or rather a woman friend, as she is no spring chicken. A black and white pup follows her everywhere, no doubt last season's effort. I keep shooing them away but to no avail. The stupid thing even wagged her tail at me and I told her that I was not friendly to her but she kept on peering at me from behind the trees, hoping for a change of heart. She's right, of course. I'm a softie. Imagine a whole pile of Salvador pups to add to the pack that roams the orchard.

Day 29

I have moved my many guests to Dood's house next door. The sausages, smelling to high heaven, were thrown out. We must have done something wrong, probably not enough salt. We didn't realize that a huge amount of salt is needed to preserve meat. Dood's house still has water and the new tenants refuse to use the toilet facilities of the orchard. I covered the previous day's dog shit with ashes from the fireplace. It's strange, but I can't tell the difference between human and dog shit.

I have been keeping a record of everyone who has been sleeping in the sitting room and have been taking super photographs by candlelight. I wonder if the flash will change the mood; shadows are weird and beautiful, like a painting by Caravaggio or de la Tour. I took a photo of Ma, Suha and Najul gossiping around the table, looking like witches. How did painters paint by candlelight? Candles shine up such a small area that they must have painted from memory. It's difficult to believe that we will have electricity again, that we will be able to turn the lights on and off at will. How one took things for granted.

There are now so many people staying here – sixteen between the two houses – that Salvador does not know who to bark at any more. He has given up. The inmates of the two houses meet for cocktails, separate for dinner and meet again for herbal teas after dinner. Cocktails are usually *arak** – the favourite drink.

A turning-point in the war. They hit a shelter, the one in Amiriya. They thought it was going to be full of party biggies but instead it turned out to be full of women and children. Whole families were wiped out. Only some of the men survived who had remained to guard their houses. An utter horror, and we don't know the worst of it yet. The Americans insist that the women and children were put there on purpose. I ask you, is

---

*   Aniseed-flavoured drink.

that logical? One can imagine the conversation at command headquarters going something like this: 'Well, I think the Americans will hit the Amiriya shelter next. Let's fill it with women and children.' What makes the Americans think they are invincible? In their very short history they've had more than their share of blunders and mistakes. Imagine my going to check up on our shelter two days before they bombed the Amiriya. Who would want to use the shelters any more? My neighbours say they now prefer to live with the noise.

The garden and orchard are beginning to dry out. I use all the washing-up water for the plants. Wish we could have a bit of rain. This morning, having a coffee with Najul in the orchard, I reminded her of another one of my pre-war dreams. In this dream, she was asking me to help her design the garden in her new house – suddenly we were in a garden full of gigantic, dried-up, cactus-like plants. I said, 'But these are all dry.' Then, 'Never mind, we'll plant a new garden.' And here we are in Dood's garden, no water, living this bizarre life. Are we now waiting for this garden to dry up?

Tonight was peaceful – after the blunder of the shelter they're laying off us for a while. Maybe now they'll have to be more careful.

Day 30
It's been one whole month. 'Read my lips.' Nobody seems to mention that fact. We are still here, ruined, and going strong. Everyone was firing in the air today. What for? Nobody knew what it was all about. Munir said dramatically that it was an invasion. In fact, it was a salute for the funeral of those who died in the shelter. I think that this firing in the air could be interpreted as a sort of indirect protest; they say that in Mosul there was an actual demonstration.

Our big mistake was not to move out of Kuwait by 15 January; that would have left the Allies in a hell of a dilemma. I wish I could see into the future – what is in store for us?

Day 31

We woke up to a totally black sky today. Who knows what they bombed. Smell of burning gasoline everywhere and a nasty, windy, sandy day. Please, rain, come and feed my plants.

We got water from the mains, and I filled every available bucket and watered some of the orchard plants. There was a peace rumour for a couple of hours; stupid people started shooting into the air, celebrating our victory. Talk about bending the facts to suit one's purpose.

I had to go to the doctor today – inflamed tonsils, throat and lungs, plus a blocked nose. He said, 'Do you smoke?' Very funny. I told him it was from our smoking chimney. At one time it was smoking so badly that visibility was down to a few metres. We couldn't understand what was happening, all of us choking away. Then Munir had a brainwave. 'Maybe the chimney's blocked,' he said. Sure enough it was. It goes to show how poorly the brains are working. Too late, though. I've been coughing non-stop for a week now. The doctor, a very nice GP, said everything was inflamed and that if I continued in this way I would become asthmatic. He plied me with many medicines. Surprisingly there were not too many people in his waiting room. One cannot afford to be ill these days – everyone has too much work to do.

The score today is 76,000 Allied air raids versus 67 Scuds.

Day 32

The scene next door in Dood's house is as follows – Najul is mother hen and everybody is under her protective wing. When the air-raid siren sounds she goes immediately to comfort her grandchildren who are scared. They all pile up around her. Everyone else follows her, her daughter, sister, brother-in-law, son-in-law; it's like a train. Najul and family share the master bedroom downstairs and Mubajal, who is totally dependent on her sister, insisted on staying close by in the dining room where she spent her time shivering with fright and cold. On the first night a large rat was found lurking in the loo nearby – Mubajal, husband and daughter quickly took their mattress and went upstairs to a small room of their own.

Salvador had a fight with some dogs today. I shooed them away but not before they had hurt his foot which is now all swollen. Poor guy. He cries when I send his girlfriends away. One is white and the other black. I feel guilty.

Ma is making an orange cake in the dark; Suha is hovering nearby and learning the process. Ma intends to bake the cake all night long on the dying embers. She thinks it will act like a slow oven. Her past efforts have been small loaves of bread, some of which have been good.

Amal fell down and bruised her nose and cheek, and broke her glasses. Now she's an even worse hazard. Amal and Munir have a thing about keys. They are permanently looking for keys which they claim to have doubles of – but the keys are always misplaced, lost or with neither of them. Two peas in a pod, those two.

We have stopped burning tyres after the BBC commented on it, and have invented a new form of camouflage – covering the bridges with poor old eucalyptus trees. They are uprooted and placed upright between sandbags. Now our bridges have wilting trees growing out of them. Apparently they are planted on bridges in the hope that their swaying will confuse the accuracy of the targeting – computers supposedly don't like moving objects! I wonder what genius thought that one up.

Day 33

I coughed all night. It rained, which was very nice. But between my coughing, the air-raid sirens and the bombing, I think I only slept about half an hour. Feeling sick. Ma's cake was burnt on the outside, raw on the inside, and tasted of smoke.

Day 34

After the rains the streets became black and shiny with great puddles that looked like oil slicks. All the black smoke descended with the rain. Are we retrieving our oil from Rumeila?

Tariq Aziz has gone to Moscow, but I don't think that will help us any. Bush is fighting a dirty war. Look what he did to Dukakis during the last campaign. He will continue to hammer us 'til the bitter end, he doesn't care how many Iraqis he kills. The West seems to have only three images of Arabs – terrorists, oil sheikhs, and women covered in black from head to toe. I'm not even sure that they know if there are ordinary human beings who live here.

Have we hit rock bottom yet, or do we still have some way to go?

Hisham came this morning to pay his condolences on Mundher's death, and to say hello. He has been in Suleimaniya all this time, apparently a lot of people went there to get away from the bombing. He was followed by Tim Llewellyn,* the first foreigner I've seen since the war began. I have cousins who are married to Brits but they have been here so long that they are tainted. One does not think of them any longer as foreign. When I saw Tim at the bottom of the drive, I literally bristled. I wonder if he felt it? I'm happy to say that by the time he'd come up our long drive I had gotten over my hostile feelings. After all, one cannot blame individuals for what their governments do. Otherwise we would all have to answer for the mess we're in, and we surely had no hand in this matter. Tim brought faxes from Sol, Dood and Charlie, our first contact with family and friends. A break in our isolation.

---

*   BBC correspondent in Iraq.

We have a new anti-aircraft gun, a 16-millimetre or whatever, very close by. It makes a beautiful, slow, dull, thud-like noise and adds weight to our nightly open-air concert. A modern symphony of sounds, discordant yet harmonious. At night, when the sky is covered with great big white, yellow and red flashes and our neighbourhood gun is thudding away, it is almost possible to fool oneself into thinking that one is attending a Philip Glass-like opera with an overlay of *son et lumière*. No *son* or even words yet, but in time it will be history, and they can have the whole of Iraq in which to play this light and sound in. Nobody agrees with my interpretation of our war music. Funnily enough, I cannot listen to any real music.

I don't like the siren. It's disturbing in its persistence. The dogs also get upset by that sound, and start barking the minute it goes off.

Well, Mr Bush said no to the overtures of Tariq Aziz. I never thought he would say yes anyway. It doesn't serve his purpose. What a brave man, he passes judgment on us while he plays golf far away in Washington. His forces are annihilating us. I find it very difficult to believe that we have been so discarded by everyone, especially the Arabs. I presume that this war will be the end of so-called Arab unity – that was a farce even while it lasted. I don't think I want to call myself an Arab any more. As an Iraqi, I can choose to be a Sumerian, a Babylonian or even an Assyrian. If the Lebanese can call themselves Phoenicians, and the Egyptians Pharaonic, why can't we follow suit?

We had a super barbecue lunch today. A lovely day, but quite noisy – the racket is still going on even now at midnight. I can't stand the Voice of America going on about American children and how they are being affected by this war. Mrs Bush, the so-called humane member of that marriage, had the gall to say comfortingly to a group of school kids, 'Don't worry, it's far away and won't affect you.' What about the children here? What double standards, what hypocrisy! Where's justice?

41

Day 35

At about 10 o'clock this morning Tim came by with a BBC retinue, saying that he wanted to do a piece about us surviving *in situ*. I talked. I don't think I was very good, didn't say any of the things I really wanted to say. I hope they edit all the dumb bits out. Then they filmed us drawing buckets of water up to the roof, and Najul and company camping in Dood's house with Jawdat lying sick in bed. I sent them off with oranges recently picked from the orchard. It will be funny if Sol and Davies see us on television.

The build-up for the land war continues. Are we capable of doing anything now? Are we to expect miracles?

Day 36

I am sitting outside typing this diary. It's a beautiful day, delicious-looking, everything clean and shining after the rains, even the oil slicks have disappeared. I've always wanted to write a book starting with this sentence: 'I live in an orchard with 66 palm trees and 161 orange trees; three male palm trees face my bedroom window, reminding me of their potency – the only males in residence. An adobe wall separates us from the neighbouring orchard.' I just typed my coffee cup off the stool with the typewriter carriage – a slapstick image from a silent movie.

We had a peaceful night last night. No air raids. The silence continues. It seems unnatural.

I can hardly believe it, but I've actually forgotten the taste of ice and of cold beer. Warm beer is getting to me. What does it matter? I only have a few bottles left.

My first anemones have come out. I bought these seeds last year in the USA. They are white. Could it be a sign of peace? Anyway, something good from the USA has grown here.

Day 37

Pat heard me on the BBC yesterday. I was called an angry woman – just as well they didn't mention my name. They didn't edit out the silly things I said, like America must be jealous of us because we have culture and they don't, and that is why they have bombed our archaeological sites. Well, who in their right minds would be jealous of us? Charlie used to tell Kiko when he was small, 'Bad luck, kid, not only were you born an Arab, but an Iraqi to boot.' What would he say now?

M.A.W. went to have lunch with Khalil, and was given Khalil's pet cock to eat. It gave him indigestion. Khalil had had this cockerel for seven years before it started to go slightly crazy and ate up two of their hens. Then he turned on the ducks. Khalil took him to the vet and the vet told him to cook him into a *tishreeb**. Imagine cooking and eating a pet you've had for seven years. It's almost like cannibalism. Khalil is so particular about his personal hygiene that he even locks his freezer just in case anyone should sneeze or cough into it and the germs pollute the goods inside.

It must have been about 9 p.m. and we were all in the kitchen washing up in the flickering candlelight after dinner. It being my turn, I'd cooked up a delicious concoction – pasta with a vodka sauce. The pasta was good, the real thing inherited from the Italian archaeologist who had rented Dood's house, and not stolen Kuwaiti stuff. Suddenly there was a terrible noise and a bright light coming closer and closer, a sun homing into us through the kitchen windows, a white, unreal daylight illuminating us all. The floor was shaking so violently that we thought the house was coming down on our heads. We crouched on the floor and suddenly, without our knowing how, the door opened and all six of us were outside in the garden. An immense fireball was hovering over us, a fireball that appeared to be burning the tops of the palm trees. Suddenly this giant

---

*   Typical Iraqi dish, made of pieces of bread with various sauces.

43

flaming object tilted, turned upwards over our heads and went roaring up into the night sky. Suha was on her knees, arms raised high, and screaming, '*Ya ustad*, why here, why in the orchards, why among our houses?' She calls Saddam *ustad** – imagine using that polite term when the world is exploding around us. We discovered later from the BBC that it was a Scud missile, launched from a mobile truck. It landed in Bahrain. At the time we couldn't decide whether it was a plane, a missile or a rocket, or even whether it was coming or going. For the first time since the war began, I thought it was all over for us. I'm sure that if its trajectory had been a few metres different we would all have been incinerated. It was like watching a rocket launch from Cape Canaveral, except this was no television and we were underneath the blast.

Immediately afterwards and while we were still outside, Ma takes me aside and whispers to me hoarsely, 'This is all your fault because you said that the Americans have no culture.' Honestly, she's quite batty sometimes. Talk about paranoia. Meanwhile, next door in Dood's house, Najul had thrown herself on top of little Zaynab, and Saysoon had thrown herself on top of them. Then Zaynab's voice was heard saying she wanted to get up. Najul said no, and the answer came back, 'In that case, I'm going to pee in my pants.' Zaynab's reaction to every air raid was to want to pee.

· At 4.30 a.m. Ma walks into my bedroom with a candle and says, 'Your radio is still on.' I wake up and start listening to it. It seems we have agreed to the Moscow initiative, but it's too late because I think the land attack started at four. I don't know what to think any more. Nobody could understand Our Leader's intentions from his speech yesterday. We took a vote at Asam's house, ten of us. The verdict ended up with three to seven in favour of withdrawal. I was one of the three who voted that he would withdraw, hoping to be right this time, so that at

---

*   Leader, teacher.

least the soldiers at the front would be saved. We have lost everything else. As usual, I was wrong.

At 5.30 I go down and make coffee for the three of us. Amal is awake and listening to the radio.

Day 38
Everyone is in a terrible depression today. Amal walked off without any breakfast when the discussion became too heated. We had to go after her. She returned with us, tight-lipped and disapproving. I think it is a bit much. We are all entitled to say what we like here. If one couldn't think and talk freely at home, then one might as well give up the ghost. It's bad enough that we can't talk outside. Needles showed up with bag and baggage, Menth carrying her bedding behind her. She had been staying at his house but has now decided to join us. Ma yelled at her and they had a fight. She said, 'That's what I've come for.'

It's a balmy day, spring is everywhere. It's difficult to believe that there is a war on. We have already had two air raids this morning, planes all over the sky. Fuzzle came by and cooked us a delicious hot lentil lunch.

Apparently last night's Scud take-off was seen and heard all over the Suleikh, and everyone thought it was directly over their heads. It was launched from somewhere near our bridge. I thought it had touched and singed the tops of the palms, it appeared that close. How and with what does one ignite (is that the right word?) a Scud? How far back does one have to stand? They seem to be horrifically inaccurate. One's mind boggles at the sheer stupidity of war.

Other people have heard me on the BBC. It has also been broadcast in the Arabic service. Amal is slightly miffed because they didn't broadcast what she said. She talked better than I did but she has such a soft voice. My well-known foghorn, as the nuns in school used to call my voice, was used instead.

If there's one thing I can't stand, it is that Bush and that horrid Rambo Schwarzkopf* will be thought of as heroes after all this is over. Will they take responsibility for the destruction and bloodshed? Their sanctimonious attitude is unbearable, as if we are the only bad guys in the world.

Air-raid sirens sound only after the planes have already come. White streaks across the sky, the sound of bombs falling and then the siren goes. I don't know why they even bother. I'm glad that this ineptitude of ours has not been publicized yet. Our ratings as the laughing stock of the world might rise even higher.

We had a barbecue dinner through the air raid, our hearts were not in it. Najul and co. have become more accustomed to the air raids and now join us in eating outside.

Day 39
Today is as ugly as yesterday was beautiful. It's misty, smoky and thick with air-raid smog. God knows what they're burning. It's noon and we've had five air raids already. My bronchial cough will not go away, which means the air is full of stuff. One can practically see it, it's that thick, least of all breathe it. Imagine what our lungs look like now. How many Hiroshimas so far? Tim Llewellyn says that the Iraqis are resigned to their fate. That is true. We're just waiting now – a few days, a few weeks. Bush and the amir of Kuwait had a breakfast date in Kuwait on the 25th. Well, it's the 25th and they're not breakfasting together yet. Small comfort.

Days 40 and 41
Nights and days full of noise, no sleep possible. What will happen to all of us now? For forty-odd days and nights – a biblical figure – we've just been standing around with our

---

*   General Norman Schwarzkopf was commander-in-chief, US Central Command, during the 1991 Gulf War.

mouths open, swallowing bombs, figuratively speaking, that is. We didn't have anything to do with the Kuwaiti take-over, yet we have been paying the price for it. Meanwhile Our Leader is alive and well – or not so well, we do not know. We're living in an Indian movie, or rather like Peter Sellers in *The Party*, refusing to die and rising up again and again, another last gasp on the bugle. In comparison, we come up every now and then with a Scud. Indian movies never really end, and I don't think this scenario will end either. If it were not such a tragedy, it would be quite funny.

Every time we do the Tarot cards with Mubajal – the Allies versus us – we get death, doom and destruction and one good survival card. The Allies get the same.

Tim came by to pick up some letters that I'm sending with him. He's leaving to go back to Cyprus. It took him ages to find me. I was pruning roses and taking cuttings in Najul's garden. Gardening is my only relief. Its therapeutic qualities are fantastic – for soothing company, nothing beats plants. If I'm feeling aggressive, I cut and prune, and when I feel hopeful I plant.

Day 42

Defeat is a rock-bottom feeling. This morning, the forty-second day, the war stopped. They kept at us all night long, just in case we had a couple of gasps left in us. It was the worst night of bombing of the whole war, relentless – nobody slept a wink. The noise was indescribable. We shook, rattled and rolled. Nobody could call this one a concert night, disharmony with no breathing spaces.

They say the Americans are in Nasiriya. Will they come to Baghdad? Like my dream, will they come marching down Haifa Street?

3 March 1991

The war has been over for some days. I lost count but for the diary which says that it lasted forty-two days. I'm sure they ended the war when they did because of the 'turkey shoot' outside Kuwait. Too much gore even for the eyes of television viewers and bad publicity for the Allies.

Today, Schwarzkopf met with whoever we sent as representatives, and we agreed to everything. After all the hyperbole that they used against us, the Americans are now simply sitting in Nasiriya and checking people's IDs. Meanwhile our national radio continues to broadcast our victorious state, it's utterly disgusting. Their line is that we fought against thirty-two nations and are still here, which is true – until one looks at the condition we're in. We are an occupied nation.

Stories of returning soldiers are endless, even the high-ranking officers are walking back from the south; total breakdown of the system. It apparently takes a week to ten days to walk the distance from Kuwait to Baghdad, all the time dodging Allied planes; the Jaguars in particular keep trying to pick off the stragglers. Who flies Jaguars other than the Brits? And they call themselves civilized, hitting at retreating and unarmed soldiers. All the wounded who could not run away fast enough got killed. The others walk with no food, no water, and simply collapse in heaps when they arrive at their houses. The whole army is in retreat and no one seems to be in command.

Stories of counterfeit money thrown from helicopters are rife in the south – presumably another way to destabilize us.

7 March

For the first time, I think there is no hope left. Life is going from bad to worse with no relief in sight. We had such a storm yesterday – wind, black sky, rain, then an orange-coloured sandstorm, then rain again, and howling wind. Two palm trees came down in Needles' orchard. They crashed on our fence, bringing it down. Now it's an easy walkover for the packs of dogs. We have killed six dogs so far, and buried them in the orchard. Now it's forbidden to use firearms, not allowed to fire a single bullet, so we have to wait for the next killings. I hate doing this, but I can't have these wild packs roaming through the garden and orchards. They're dangerous and destructive.

Sections of Baghdad already have electricity. Some say we will get it tomorrow. I don't believe it. It apparently comes for a day and then goes off. I'm sure they are trundling the same generator round to different parts of Baghdad to give everybody a taste of electricity. I've forgotten what it feels like to switch a light on.

Rumour has it that Basra has fallen again. It seems Iranians are in there fighting, swarthy guys in *sharwals*.* Too many rumours not to believe there is some truth in them.

8 March

Just returned from a yummy lunch of smoked salmon. You might well ask from where? Lubna gave me some before the war, and I stored it with Abbas who had a generator. Withdrew it today, and ate it at Dhafir and Mutaza's. They had electricity and I consumed my first bit of ice in ages. Mutaza says that electricity shows up the dirt in your house. Ever since hers came on, she has been cleaning like a demented woman. I dread to think what my house is going to look like, all that soot from the chimney must have left a thick film on everything. Better to stay in the dark. I kept the shutters down throughout to protect the windows, so it was dark even during the day.

9 March

I had a nightmare last night. I was holding a little carving, a beautiful white Sumerian head with ruby eyes. Someone, an Iraqi, maybe Fulayih, broke it while trying to pierce it – I think he was trying to turn it into a bead. Then Fulayih's father comes

---

*   Baggy trousers.

into the kitchen and I tell him about my dream. He throws up on the table. I rush out crying, to find a mass of dogs in the orchard, but am too sad to shoo them away.

I hope everyone who had a hand in this disastrous mess falls into the burning oilwells. How can one live with so much hypocrisy?

The Soviets say that they never expected us to go to war with the USA and so did not give us their latest and best equipment, only what was adequate to fight with our Third World neighbours. I wonder if that was the truth or just a cover-up, an excuse for their inferior weaponry.

10 March
It is 10.30 at night and I have five candles burning in my room. What an extravagance. Hopefully we'll be getting electricity soon. Life is becoming boring. Before we at least had the excitement of the air raids and the bombing fireworks. Now there is silence and a humdrum existence. By the time one has filled up the bottle candles with kerosene, cleaned the lamps and the grate, picked up the day's fallen oranges in the orchard, swept and cleaned the house, gathered firewood, and thrown a few stones at roaming dogs, the day is over. I sold 52 kilos of oranges today for 1162 dinars.

There is no petrol, no electricity, no running water and no telephone.

Hala was very funny today, ranting and raving about how she has missed out on life, no future, to die a virgin ... yelling hysterically at her mother, 'At least you have your husband to sleep with!' Nothing but bleakness looms ahead, certainly not a fancy love life. In the streets one sees lots of men but our houses are full of women. There are so few men in our lives.

I have been saying all along that Bush and Saddam are alike. They both carried out their threats. They bombed and we burned. Now Bush is also handing out medals; soon he will be giving away cars as presents. His speeches are now studded with heavy, sycophantic clapping. History, I think, will not see Bush as a hero but as a destroyer. We are a Third World country, well known for not having too much common sense. Why could he not have negotiated a peace instead of an annihilation? Just look at what has been done to the environment.

11 March

Talk about being buried alive. We may as well not exist. Nobody talks to us. No news about us. Only rumours thrive.

My first iris opened today.

Ma and Needles got their windows repaired; 305 dinars to replace three bloody bits of glass, a shattering expense – pun intended. Poor Amal paid thousands of dinars to replace the glass in her house and shop. Maybe we should send the repair bills to the US president who 'has no fight with the Iraqi people'.

Riding my bike back tonight from dinner at Suha's, the streets were black and empty. No moon; silence but for the drone of a few generators.

12 March

They say there are tanks placed between the houses in Nasiriya, bulldozing people and everything in sight. Sounds like civil war. Ma and Najul had made a pact that if things remained the same after the end of the war, they would commit suicide together. They have now changed their minds. They say it's not worth it.

Sheikha said that the Western media exaggerated and fantasized us to be this great and mighty power, the fourth largest army in the world, and that we actually believed it. We went into the war convinced and certain about the strength of our glorious army, that conclusion based only on Western propaganda. We fell for their line, how stupid can we get? Sheikha says that it's because we instantly believe compliments, it's one of our major weaknesses as a people.

Many macabre and funny stories going around town. One about a taxi-driver coming back from the front with a dead soldier's coffin strapped on top of his car. He was searching for the poor bugger's parents and went into a house to ask the way; comes out to find his taxi and the coffin gone. There are no police to complain to. Another story is about a government truck selling gas canisters in the street; when they'd all been sold and the driver was ready to move off, he discovered there was no petrol in the car. It had all been siphoned out. Thievery is the order of the day. Sheikha says that the only thing the West knows about us is the fable of *The Thief of Baghdad*. Maybe there is some truth to that story.

Nofa has accumulated over 100 empty gas canisters in her garage because someone promised her a lorryload of full ones. In the meantime, the boys in the neighbourhood are extracting a sort of petrol out of the gas dregs at the bottom. Every five gas canisters produces about a litre of this 'petrol'. Smart alecks who do not mind ruining their cars are using it. It has left a reeking smell in the garage which has lasted for days, and it is driving Asam crazy. The lorry has not materialized.

Went to my grocery shop today to pick up rations for the month. Tahsin, the shopkeeper, told me that he had heard me talk on the BBC. He asked me what it was like outside, in the UK. I couldn't think of much to say except that it rains so much there that your bones get wet. He thought a minute and then said, 'I guess every place has its pros and cons.' A sweet chap. His mother Khairiya, a lovely, smiling lady, took literacy classes and came first, but now she says that she can't read a thing. She forgot it all – she failed in religion. She wants to start classes again after the war. Ma's and Needles' maid also had to take those classes, but after three years she was unable to read even bus numbers. Even so, those literacy classes did teach.

Munir crashed into a pole while on his bike and smashed his face and nose.

13 *March*

We had the black clouds with us again today and it rained. What are we breathing? All our houses are streaked with huge black drips, dripping from the parapets of the roofs. It's the new fringed look. We might start a fashionable trend in external house patterning.

No changes in our lives. Only rumours, which one can take or leave.

Abu Ali came today and we decided to build the *tanoor** that I'd bought. He encased it in mud and plastered it with plaster that we found in the garage. The top surface was finished with turquoise tiles from Karbala and the sides were decorated with some old glazed tiles which Ma had bought. One was from Karbala, another from Kufa, two from Hamza and one from Abu Hanifa – a real cross-section of sects – a holy *tanoor*. We smoked it carefully the first day, firing it slowly so that it would not crack. An old dustbin lid works well as a cover. It looks lovely. As of tomorrow we can cook bread and cakes in our own *tanoor*.

14 *March*

What a way to raid a country! Apparently we denuded Kuwait of everything plus the kitchen sink. Aeroplanes, buses, traffic lights, appliances, everything. Shops all over the country are full of their consumer goods. Imagine!

We know, and learn nothing new about our situation.

We may have petrol by Sunday. Bush says he's worried about the mess we're in – how decent of him.

I wish I'd kept a diary in the six months before the war started when we had that endless array of dignitaries coming to visit, starting with Waldheim and ending with de Cuellar. Then there was always hope. Now, nine months later, we're a beaten

---

*   Clay oven.

nation. We are told to rebel by the West, with what and how? I must do something or go mad. Build a swimming pool?

16 March

Yesterday Suha got electricity. M.A.W. passed by and said they were all meeting there, including N. Imagine seeing N. as the first face with electricity. I chose not to. Instead, M.A.W. came here and we played cards. He's always complaining that I cheat because I peer into his hands. What difference does that make when I can never remember what I've seen anyway? He still holds out his cards right in front of my face. He can't see too well by candle and lamplight – not my fault.

More irises are out.

It was deadly quiet during the day because the security forces were out checking for arms in houses in the Grey'at area near us. They searched Khalil's and Amal's houses. They took away Khalil's typewriter even though he has permission for it. I wonder if I should hide mine? He was very upset with the officers because they fingered everything, including his wife's underwear. I asked him how he could have eaten his favourite pet cockerel, and told him that I thought it was cannibalistic. He said that he'd been feeling so guilty about the whole episode that he'd been having disturbed dreams about him for days.

17 March

The stories are getting more grotesque. Kufa, Kirkuk and Basra – bodies and bodies lying everywhere. In Kufa it seems they have pillaged the university buildings and burned papers and documents in the library.

18 March

I had an endless stream of visitors today at the studio, Assia and Suha included. The bombing had been so bad near them that they spent the entire time on the floor of the laundry room, all piled up together, sharing the space with a large rat who delivered a litter in the midst of them, so she says. It was the only room in the house that didn't have outside windows and they felt safe there. All their windows went, all that expanse alongside the river across from the Dora refinery. Said S. also came by, riding on his bike dressed in an impeccable white linen suit with a bottle of lemon juice in one pocket, a bottle of vodka and a glass in the other. An eccentric sight in Baghdad. He gave us a good explanation of why one has to keep fridge and freezer doors shut. If the doors are left open, the seal dries and cracks and can no longer function properly. Whether the appliance is off or on is immaterial.

The Mansur gang have run out of petrol, that is why we haven't seen them for a week. We were worried enough to go for a visit. Lubna regaled us with many stories about robberies in their area, apparently the hot favourites are now chandeliers. Does someone have a chandelier shop that needs restocking, or is someone collecting enough to open a store?

Our situation is not getting any better.

19 March
In the coffee shops the talk is not of nationalism, but of the desire for the US to come in and take over – get it over with. Saddam still appears on television. I suppose the powerful must feel naturally immune. Hasn't history, especially our violent one, taught them anything?

20 March
I was on my bike going to pick up some bread when a white van starts hooting frantically at me. It was Mir and Ilham signalling me. I haven't seen them since the first night of the war. They came back to Baghdad a few weeks into the war and remained. Her father died the day of the first black rain and none of us even knew about it. They had a macabre time trying to get him buried, finding a priest for the last rites, finding a taxi to take

them to the cemetery, even finding a man to dig the grave – a horror story. We had similar problems when we had to bury Mundher Baig.

A gang robbed Umberto's house of 1,000 crates of beer which he was storing for his company. Only his clothes and the beer were taken. Each crate sells for 80 dinars – that's 80,000 dinars right there: a fortune. No one steals electrical goods any more except for chandeliers. Petrol, beer and cigarettes are the popular items. Oddly enough, they all go for the same price.

It seems we will be allowed to travel from 1 June. Human rights dictates that people can travel and we must follow those guidelines. Human rights?

Many days later, 28 March
It is too depressing to write. One keeps on saying that it can't get worse and it does. How much worse can it get?

I went with Nofa to Salman Park. She had to go and see about the orchards there. I found a whole field of those dandelion-like flowers, puff balls; when we were kids we used to blow on them and make a wish. I tried it three times. Every time I wished to know when all this would end. But there were always some tufts left clinging on. I counted them: seventeen altogether. Does that mean seventeen days, weeks, months or years? I say seventeen months is how long it will last, or could it be years? God forbid.

Met Muhammad G.'s sister today, recently fled from Karbala. She saw horrific sights, dead bodies left on the street, their relatives too frightened to remove them. Bodies being eaten by dogs and cats. They've been bulldozing the area around the mosque and shrines; people were given three days to clear out of their houses. All of old Karbala will disappear. The whole thing is sick.

I have a new war on, a war against snails. At least 10 billion snails have invaded the orchard – the round figure that's being bandied around for everything these days. It might as well apply to my snail count. They eat every green thing they see. They even ate my new baby magnolia tree, transplanted recently from Asam's garden. She says these things only happen in my garden, never hers. The dogs are on the increase again. Poor Salvador. He has to pee so much to mark his territorial boundaries that his leg is permanently poised in mid-air. He's quite exhausted and may be dehydrated.

We came back walking tonight, pushing our bikes. Nearly a full moon. Naila only found out her brother was alive when Yaki saw him on television in London, a hostage in Saudi Arabia – live on CNN, as they say.

2 April
I have decided to build a swimming pool. So when Abu Ali came by today I told him about it and he says he will find me some diggers.

5 April
Abu Ali came marching in with four strapping six-footers, spades in hand. They drew an outline in white chalk in the back garden between the two houses and immediately started to dig in with terrific force. In fact, a frenzy that I've never seen in Iraqi workmen.

10 April
In four days I had a hole measuring 8 x 4 metres with a depth slanting from 1 to 2 metres. A mountain of earth on the sides. They said it was not their business to remove it. I am now the proud owner of a large hole in the ground and feel much the better for it. The bad news is there is no cement, or the little there is of it is being used for government reconstruction projects. None of us had even thought of that. Imagine forgetting so soon that most factories had been bombed to smithereens.

Our mail is working more smoothly now that Freako, good old Freako, is acting as go-between in Jordan. Excellent service, mainly done through taxi-drivers going back and forth between Amman and Baghdad. She sends on letters, faxes, as well as goodies and newspapers. What a treat. That's about all I can read now. I still can't listen to music, but have started to paint again. I don't know why I couldn't work during the war. Seen carried on painting and listening to music throughout. The same thing happened to me during the civil war in Beirut. That's why I had to leave there. In wartime my creative process simply dries up, the destructiveness around is so soul-destroying.

15 April
Tragedy. I thought there was something wrong with the film in my camera that never seemed to finish. When I bravely opened the camera in the dark, there was no film. What sorrow and horror! How am I going to get another war again? On second thoughts, at the rate we're going, we may have another quite soon. We have no proof of what we went through now. All those unbelievable images. Gone.

That is where my diary ended. I must add a few things. I can't understand how I forgot to write about them at the time.

After the war ended, the Allies spent all day and all night flying over our heads and breaking the sound barrier. Just like in Panama when they blasted Noriega, holed up in the Vatican embassy, with music. For fifteen days, Bush deafened the poor ambassador and Noriega with hard rock. Our torture went on for months – twenty or thirty times, day and night, jets broke the sound barrier over our heads, horrific deafening noise, swooping down, rubbing our noses in the dirt. As if we hadn't had enough noise and dirt. The Israelis used to do this to us in Beirut – a daily, though not nightly, occurrence for years.

On 26 April, Sol opened the door and walked in on Ma and Needles as they were having their afternoon nap, each on a chair. I didn't see her 'til five hours later. I was gadding about seeing friends. Always said that she would be the first one to brave coming back to Baghdad after the war. Our contact with the outside world was somehow reconnected.

Bush says he has nothing against the Iraqi people. Does he not know or realize that it is only the Iraqi people who have suffered? It's us, and only us, who've been without electricity and water – a life of hardship.

I am sending this to my sister in New York.

Baghdad, June 1991

Baghdad Diaries

P.S. – August 1992, Frenchman's Bay, Maine

I sent two copies of this diary to Sol. They both got lost in the mail. It's a good thing that Ma had made three photocopies. The third time it arrived safely – that was in January 1992. Was it the notorious US mail service or did I just put the wrong postal code? I swore that I would not come to the West again, but I was nagged into it by Sol – life must go on, as she says. Everybody who knows Sol knows how determined she can be. Letters were written, and visas obtained. Long queues, humiliation, no country wants us. We are the pariahs of the world.

When I first arrived in London, I felt sad and distant. With the drama of the war over, no one seemed interested or even aware of our tragic situation. The papers only write about the Kurds or about the UN inspections.

Now I'm in Maine, staying with Sol and the Doc. A family reunion: Ma, Kiko, all of us together, only Dood and family missing. We are editing the diary; Sol is chief editor.

The reconstruction process in what is left of Iraq has been dramatic – most utilities, factories, buildings and bridges that were bombed have been rebuilt with true Iraqi ingenuity. Even if a lot of it was true Third World jerry-rigging, we did it ourselves with no help from the outside world. But the social system has suffered. Inflation, counterfeit money, poverty and hunger are the order of the day. There are shortages of everything – medicine, food, spare parts – though most things can be had for a price. Medical and social services are in a mess. Burglaries are now a common occurrence and Baghdad, once a 'safe' city to live in, is safe no longer.

I am returning to Baghdad in September. The second anniversary of the Kuwait invasion has just passed and war cries are sounding again. It all sounds too familiar.

Embargo

3 November 1994 – Baghdad
The first thing I noticed coming into Baghdad at four in the morning, after being away for ten months, was how wide, clean and well-looked-after the main streets were. I'd forgotten that. Naturally, there wasn't a soul on them. At the border they took a blood sample for an AIDS test, luckily with a disposable needle. The guards at the border looked well fed, but they still wanted something to eat. Heard a few good stories – the best about a woman who took a whole cooking pot full of drugged or poisoned *dolma** as a present to the guards of the Abu Hanifa mosque. While the guards slept, the whole place was robbed – carpets, chandeliers, everything. It took one of the guards two days to wake up – imagine the quantity that was administered.

Salvi wasn't around when I arrived at the house. He came later and leapt all over me, crying and whining. He had two friends with him – the old faithful black lady and a young, odd-looking Alsatian with a very short tail sort of tucked into his hind legs. Salvi never did have good taste in dogs.

Hashim says he'll give my car to a friend who will renew the licence – that's what he did for his own car. He gave him 1,000 dinars and a bucket of yoghurt. A strange combination. My telephone is naturally out of order and there are moths flying all

---

*   Stuffed vegetables.

over the storeroom, even though it reeks so badly of moth balls that I could scarcely breathe.

4 November

A lot of talk about food and prices. An egg costs 60 dinars – even during the war a dozen eggs only cost 4 dinars! My new car battery is going to cost 16,000 dinars. Cars crawl round the streets of Baghdad, their tyres as smooth as babies' bottoms – not a ridge left on them. People are living by stealing and cheating. Leila and Hatem had all four tyres stolen. Their car was propped up on bricks and parked at their front door – the thieves also took their washing off the line in the garden. Jassim's ex-nanny, who now works at the 'palace', says they keep the staff on starvation rations and watch them like hawks in case they steal (or use poison, I added). She said that when someone was caught stealing, they gathered the staff together, brought in a doctor who chopped off this guy's hand, and immediately dunked it into boiling oil to cauterize it.

6 November

This year's war is against worms and caterpillars: black striped, grey-green, horrid things – millions of them everywhere. Nature is odd; how come worms are thriving while people starve? I'm killing them by the dozens. Horrid green mush oozes out. They're riddling the garden with holes. I have been homebound because the car is battery-less though a battery has been bought. An Iranian battery costs 24,000 dinars (which is what I will have), a Turkish one 18,000, while an Iraqi one costs 12,000 – I can't remember what a Korean one costs. It's pot luck how long any one of them lasts. I can use my car only in this neighbourhood, otherwise I can be fined 2,000 dinars because I don't have a numbered sticker on my car. A new law came into existence in my absence that stated that Japanese cars had to have a number etched on them, like cattle. I'm surprised that they haven't started doing that to Iraqis – a stamp on our foreheads would be most fetching. Better not to even think of such an idea or someone with a sixth sense will pick it up and before we know it, it will be law, then God help us.

Said rented out a room in their *khan* for two trays of eggs a month – a contract was signed, stamped and legalized! Quite clever of him. The tenant is now losing money as the price of eggs rises ever upwards. Mu'taza's mum said she asked the people renting her house for one chicken a year. They refused – imagine not even being able to afford one chicken. How can one not be resentful about the situation? Today at Ma and Needles, we were suddenly eight people at lunchtime and there wasn't enough reserve to feed them – so we just sat. No wonder people are not going out – they can't afford to repay hospitality. Ma said the freezer only had dates and flour. All the talk was of a TV movie that was shown a couple of weeks ago about a bunch of special recruits?/soldiers? leaping on a small wolf or dog, tearing him to bits and eating the liver. No one seems quite certain of the purpose or message of this film – to scare people? It's not a new film.

7 November
Tariq Aziz is called 'Tariq '*Aza*' by the Christians in Baghdad – *aziz* means dear but '*aza* means mourning. Today there was another bomb scare in a Christian children's school in Karrada. I wonder if it's the fundamentalists getting at the remaining Christians. It always seems to be in that same area.

8 November
Paolo says three Scuds hit Abu Ghuraib today and broke all the windows in their Haifa Street Institute – there has been no official acknowledgment of the attack.

We went to get vegetables from Jamila – sacks in hand. It's cheaper this way and we share them between three households. Assia was sneezing and blowing her nose in a strange flowered rag. 'Yes,' she says, 'write that down. I don't have the money to buy Kleenex and am using Zaynab's doll's dress as a hankie. This is the embargo.' Mind you, she spends at least 200 dinars a day on cigarettes – her priority in life. Jamila was a sea of mud and slush. Assia had a hole in the top of her clogs, and as she waded through it, a jet of liquid mud shot out of the top of her clogs.

Salvi brought his son to me today: black with a white dot on the bum. They all take after their mum. He was trying very hard to ingratiate himself with me, grinning wildly and wagging his short tail. He dumped a dead chicken by the car. I'm not certain whether Salvi kills them, or finds them dead and brings them back as an easy trophy. I have never seen him in action.

9 November
Went and ate fish in Abu Nawas Street with the Italians at night, streets full of little kids aged from five to twelve, selling Chiclets and shining shoes – sad, haggard, forlorn and listless faces.

If one deposits money in the banks these days, they weigh it in bundles. People go in and out all day with gunny sacks in their hands – if the bank tellers had to physically count these millions, they'd only be able to manage four customers a day. It is really funny-looking, photocopy money.

Latest Saddam joke going round the *souq*: in a meeting he asks his ministers what the time is; someone answers, 'Whatever time you say, sir.'

11 November
People are being warned by their doctor friends against having an operation in Baghdad. The anaesthetic is bad. It makes the patient hysterical on waking up. The embargo has been on against Cuba for thirty-five years. God forbid that we have to wait that long – I would love to go there and compare notes.

12 November

Muayad is cross with me for saying he has a big stomach in my diary. 'I can't help it if you have a big stomach,' I said. While waiting for Paolo to finish his papers at the museum, an employee there starts telling me about a retarded nephew of his who disappeared for a week. Yesterday the army called them up and told them that they had him and that he was listed as a deserter. They threatened to chop off an ear if they didn't come and show proof that he was exempted from being in the army. Anyone who catches a deserter gets 10,000 dinars, so all types are getting caught up in the mess.

Met some new relatives today. We live two streets apart but have never heard of them. We might be coming into wads of money. This dynamic, slim and elegant lady with beautiful fingers has come across a huge lot of property that we have inherited from a great-grandmother. It's an hour away from Baghdad, in a place called Sultan Abd al-Hamid, and is supposedly the most fertile land in the whole of Iraq. This cousin, accompanied by two carloads of government officials that she had brought along, marched into these usurped orchards and laid claim to them. I told her that she had better go in disguise when they auction them. 'Not on your life,' she said. 'I'm not scared.' I can well believe that. Needles was busy filling her in on the historical background of the family and who's who in it. Ma will go with this cousin to follow up on this new source of wealth.

Needles spent a day making a portable cupboard out of old curtains. She had an old plastic one that was beginning to fall apart, so she took the frame apart and hung it with recycled old curtains. Everyone is recycling everything.

Told Salvi that he had received a fan letter from Canada. Sol told me about it over the phone. I haven't seen it yet. Anyway, I think he purred and scratched at a few flea bites. The streets around us are full of baby Salvis – he has been active. He's most

keen on blackie with white dot on bum, they play like father
and son.

13 November

Hatra.* The entire landscape has changed – walls and columns
stamped with his initials, everywhere concrete. They could have
left Hatra alone, it was so wonderful. They ruined Babylon but
in reality there was nothing left to ruin. Dinner at the Hatra
Hotel; nouvelle cuisine – five bits of very charcoaled meat, three
slices of tomato and three small triangles of bread for 4,000
dinars. My Toyota Corona cost that much in 1981. Moon so
bright we couldn't see the stars. Iraqi dogs have proprietary
rights to the archaeological sites – each group with its own area
– and terrible wars go on between them. They chased me away.

14 November

Hatra. This morning at dawn I walked through the temple area,
the stone pink and luminous in the early light. Dogs lounging on
the steps saw me, a lone tourist, and started up the most terrific
racket, echoes everywhere. Went on to Mosul, Nimrud and
Nineveh, where we were taken to see the new winged bulls
discovered on Nabi Younis – a most distressing sight. These
wonderful and majestic stone carvings, broken and scattered in
pieces all over the place – people have been stealing bits, kids
are breaking off fragments. The place is full of robber holes.
Nimrud is a little better, although the carved exposed steles are
also eroding and breaking up. We visited the royal tombs of the
wives of the Assyrian kings which had contained wonderful
gold objects and jewellery. I had my little Beirut hand torch with
me so I was able to climb down and look at them – a really
exciting and weird sensation. So clean and neat, as if they were
built and tended with lots of love and care. The guard said that

---

*   Ancient archaeological site: Saddam Hussein has had his initials
        carved on some of the stone and marble slabs.

he had found the first tomb (I'm not sure that I believe him, although he was there) and that it was spotless, no dirt anywhere, just kilos of gold! I asked him whether he ever dreams of the ancient inhabitants or tries to communicate with them, and he said no, they are all gone – not much imagination there. The tombs are on such a human scale – unlike the more grandiose Egyptian ones – that one can easily relate to them.

15 November

Everyone seems to be dying of cancer. Every day one hears about another acquaintance or friend of a friend dying. How many more die in hospitals that one does not know? Apparently over thirty percent of Iraqis have cancer, and there are lots of kids with leukaemia. They will never lift the embargo off us. Saddam appeared on TV this evening, stating that Albright's[*] speech was a pack of lies. Nothing is in my name, he said, it's all for the state. True enough, he doesn't need to put anything in his name. The whole country is his.

Thamina, as usual, wonderfully funny with her throw-away remarks, talking about immigration – everyone is leaving, she said, and we were never a country of immigrants. Now you can't even find a first-rate prostitute in town, they too have gone. I asked her how she knew that. She said, 'Look at the terrible singers we now get on TV!' Twenty-one members of her family have left, only eight remain in Baghdad. Her daughter said that a lot of kids have stopped going to school, the parents can't afford to buy exercise books and pencils. A friend of hers who lives in Mansur told her that her thirteen-year-old daughter had locked herself in her room crying because she wanted to walk down the main shopping street and her mother said no. 'I can't afford to let her,' she said. 'Everything costs in the thousands. I can barely afford to give them a sandwich to take

---

[*]   Madeleine Albright was the US ambassador to the United Nations.

to school.' This is a middle-class family living in a good neighbourhood, and reasonably well off.

There is a popular song on TV which is constantly being requested. It shows a boy lying down dying on his bed: he has just cut out his kidneys and is handing them out for love – it sounds grotesque. I hate TV and never watch it, but I must look out for this true-love scene. We are weird even when showing our ardour.

17 November

Abu Ali passed by today. He has two sons in the army now. One is in a military prison because he was so hungry he went home to eat, but was caught as a deserter and locked up for three months. The army doesn't feed or clothe its soldiers any more. The other son, Ahmed, is out in the middle of nowhere guarding an arms depot. Poor Abu Ali, he looks worn out. He has tried to get his sons out of the army but has been unable to do so; it's a presidential decree that all young men should be in the army. It has been raining for the past two days, just pouring. Naturally, the telephone isn't working. I keep rushing out to the garden to check on my seedlings, to see if they've been drowned. Some are beaten to a pulp, others have emerged but are in heavy disarray.

Salvi is a little ill, maybe with a cold. He won't eat and his stomach makes noises as if he's swallowed something live – perhaps that's how dog gasses sound. He looks miserable. His black son came by to visit and he walked him to the gate, came back and plonked himself in a heap on his blanket.

Went and visited Fulayih, who has just spent four months in jail; he said it was frightful and wished he'd been in for murder rather than for stealing.

'How could you say that?' I asked.

'Well,' he said, 'if one has to be had up for something, with us Arabs it's more honourable to kill than to steal.'

Something strange is happening – little business enterprises are being started by seemingly ordinary individuals who take your money, invest it, and promise a 30–70 percent profit in a month. It starts off well enough, and the first investors duly get their profits. Slowly word gets round and more and more people put in their money, quantities of money, some even sold their houses and valuables. All this without a paper changing hands, your name is simply written in a ledger. After a few months, the government clamps down, the person running the enterprise is put into jail, the money is confiscated and the investors lose everything. My theory is that the government is in on it – it's a government mafia scam organized to steal from the people. After all, they have the printing machines to print out the money, they can afford to hand out a few thousands and then collect them and the people's money too. They may even pay the salaries of their civil servants with this money. One of these enterprises belongs to the wife of one of Saddam's bodyguards – they even advertise it on TV. Perhaps this is their way of curbing rampant inflation! The latest joke circulating round Baghdad goes as follows. A guy is stopped on the streets by a beggar asking for money. The guy answers, 'Go to Sam Co. [the latest enterprise to have crashed], they have my money.' The beggar answers, 'They have mine too.'

The other day at Fuzzle's house I met a lady who had a miserable story to tell. Her husband had worked for Iraqi Airways and was pensioned off after the war, when flying out of Iraq was banned by the UN. Apparently, they had been building a house that was nearing completion when it was robbed – light fittings, doors, bathroom fixtures, windows, everything that could be lifted was lifted. The landlord of the house they were renting wanted them out and took them to court; the judge was in the landlord's pay and he won the case. So this poor family was forced to move into the shell of their new house. They boarded up the windows and doors with cardboard since they couldn't afford windows or doors. They wrote a petition to the government to explain their case, and the answer came back informing them that even though this particular judge was caught on bribery and corruption charges and had been put in jail, they couldn't pass a judgment on his judgment. The poor woman is going crazy, her husband does nothing all day long. He shouts at her, she just cries.

Can't use a normal-sized purse any longer; the quantity of money that one has to carry round means plastic bags, like Italian money used to be.

A strange abnormality – many babies are being born dumb. It's probably better for them that way: they won't have a chance to talk against anything.

25 November
There are three generations of Salvi's offspring barking outside. I can't think what has gotten into them. They have been in and out all day. I shoo them away and see another lot coming from the other side. Perhaps they're visiting him on his sickbed. He is still not well. Majeed made me cook some garlic for Salvi today, and he seems better for it.

Saw Faiza today. She said she'd like a catastrophe to envelope the USA and swallow the whole continent.

'What about my two brothers who live there?' her husband Mahmood asked.

'They can go down with it,' she said. 'Serve them right for living there.' Hatred for the USA is paramount here.

The Suleikh is nothing but women. Every home has only women. Where are the men, the husbands, brothers and uncles? Could they all be dead? Women are supposed to be the tougher sex.

27 November
Everyone is talking about the fall of Sam Co. They showed them on TV, a young man – a hairdresser – and his two

unprepossessing partners. One wouldn't give them a tenner, let alone all one's possessions. People are kicking themselves over their stupidity. More and more I think it's a government trick.

Salvi is still ill and sleeps all day. After he eats he barks a bit and then collapses onto his blanket. Am beginning to worry.

28 November

Tim called. He is here to make a TV film on the embargo. Got Ma and Needles over, lit a fire and offered a few things to nibble on. My freezer has coffee and nuts from Amman, a few bones for Salvi and ice for me, so they got meagre offerings. They're waiting for permission to start filming.

29 November

There were twenty to twenty-five ladies for tea at Ma's, a number of them wearing red – including the largest in size, who never stopped talking. It seems that she was a wild thing in her youth, left her husband and ran off with her afternoon lover, married him and has lived happily ever since. Assia and Suha came late. Assia wants to write a book about sex and Islam so that she can become famous and seek asylum in Sweden. She was blowing her nose in a white towel today. She said it used to be a massage towel from times gone by when she indulged in massages.

I've had a rat in my studio for the past three days. I've given him/her two kinds of poisoned sandwiches. It eats the bread and leaves the filling behind. I'm having my third try today. If it doesn't work, then Suhair is giving me a trap that gets three at one go. The mind boggles. What sort of trap could it be, and is it likely that three rats would wait together to be trapped?

No call from Tim. I guess they don't have a permit yet. Rabab showed up from Amman with some mail. She says that the USA's behaviour is even more amoral than ours. It's predetermined, and only hurts the poor. More stories about burglaries, this time in the embassy of Qatar – the thieves went into the house, piled all the stuff into a lorry and made the consul drive his car ahead of them to show the guards that the move was with his permission. They got away.

30 November
Went with the girls to see Hajir. House full of photographs, mementoes, albums. We looked at a lot of old and new photos of births, marriages, and the kids growing up, followed by endless conversations about whose mother was who. A lot of the Jamil family ladies seem to start thinking about genealogies at eleven at night or later, and start phoning each other up, asking who was so-and-so's mother – making lists. Hajir says it's a sign of senility in their family.

1 December
Tim arrived with his crew at about 10.30. Filmed a scene with him arriving at the gate, ringing the bell and kissing me hello. Salvi went hysterical, barking all day and trying to bite everybody. Had to repeat the shoot because there was too much barking on the sound track. He certainly won't get any more fan letters after this show. I managed to get a collar on him. (We will have to tie him up on Saturday when they come to take my kilns away – the end of an era.) I think they got enough filming done.

3 December
Well, my kilns have gone. I don't know what to feel. They went on top of a rickety lorry that had to be pushed to start it. Before they left, the chief Kurdish mover told me to call on them if I ever needed anything. I said, 'What's your name?'

He said, 'Muhammad Kassim, like the superhighway.'

I said, 'I'll not forget it.'

'That's right,' he said, and he leaped onto the now-moving lorry and went off waving. I am left feeling insecure – I have been wedded to the old kiln for the last thirty years. I didn't feel any pangs for the new kiln. Too late to get sentimental. We finally found the rat, which turned out to be a mouse. It must have died last night after eating the poisoned meat I left for it. When they lifted the kiln we found her nest (she must have been expecting). Beside it was a collection of little objects – a blue bead, a little light bulb 2 centimetres long that must have been part of the signal light at the back of the kiln, a couple of film spools and a button. What could she have been doing? Collecting toys for her future babies? I felt really sorry, and have kept the nest – it's very neat and cushiony and built of insulating material from the air-conditioner.

I decided to start something new so I got out the new typewriter ribbon that Sol had such difficulty finding for me in New York. It has a white correction strip that does not seem to be working. Maybe I put it in wrong. Had to tie up Salvi; he's got a new yellow rope – I bribed him with a bit of food. He has to get used to being tied up again in the morning, otherwise everyone will refuse to come through the front gate. Janette has taken to parking her car on her lawn so it's visible and somewhat safer from thieves, she hopes. I think I've been back a month. The first japonica bloomed today – I'm looking on it as an omen, an OK sign for me to have sold off my kilns. After reading *Zen and the Art of Motorcycle Maintenance*, my kiln became my friend. It is much travelled, too, even though it weighs a ton. I feel a pang of regret.

8 December

In one day everything got frozen over, three degrees below zero. Mosul is six below – only Moscow is colder. Paolo just came and borrowed my big Syrian coat – no one is prepared for this cold, which is at least three weeks early. My little plants have shrivelled up. No electricity since six this morning. It's now 5.30 in the afternoon. Something terrible must have happened. I'll have to return to a freezing cold house tonight. The gas heater is on, it's dark and I'm typing by an old war gaslight. It's good that I've kept them functioning. It feels just like wartime minus the noise. My telephone goes off every time it rains and when it's very cold. There are also long periods when it switches off. I think they rotate the exchanges, thus preserving the parts. There are none to spare.

It cost me 2,675 dinars to have my car number scratched on the front and back windows of my car. Apparently Japanese cars are stolen with such ease that this is a way of controlling the number against the certificate of ownership. To check if the name and number tally on the computer costs 5,000 dinars – so if it's stolen, the name of the thief won't tally with the number. It makes wonderful sense, but who will pay 5,000 dinars for that information? I paid a 2,000-dinar fine because I was not there when my car number was called. I showed them my passport and told them that I was out of the country on that date, but they said fines for car numbers cannot be cancelled. In fact, they purposely delay the papers so that everybody ends up having to pay the fine. They scratched the numbers and stuck a badge that had UK protection, 100 D, written on it. No doubt these badges were stolen from Kuwait. The whole procedure is quite mystifying. And why only Japanese cars? All sorts of cars are being stolen these days.

11 December

Attended a conference on the after-effects of the war on the environment. An archaeological conference was going on at the same time but it was closed to the public. Muayad gave me the cold eye, staring straight through me. Donny also walked by and totally ignored me. They both still have protruding stomachs although Muayad's is now smaller. Lunch with Bernard, the mad scientist, and we were joined by another mad scientist, a French princess called Isabel, who never stopped talking. She's a specialist on the environment, in particular the aftermath of wars and nuclear fallout (she spent many weeks in Chernobyl after the explosion). Although all sorts of statistics are being gathered on Iraq, scientists need seven years of observation before they can be positive about the accuracy of their data. Baghdad and Basra got the worst of the bombing in an operation called Watertap when the USA experimented with Barite (is that correct?) bombs. Apparently, these do not make a big bang but just let out a lot of smoke. Some die immediately from its effects, others linger on for years. They were experimenting. In years to come, history will show how destructive the West's policy was towards us. At the morning session, two Dutch scientists said that the Gulf War was an exercise undertaken intentionally to destroy the infrastructure of Iraq.

While Isabel and I were talking, an Iraqi journalist came up to me and asked me whether I was Japanese.

I said, 'Do I look Japanese?'

'No,' he said. 'Where do you come from?' All the while I've been talking to him in Arabic. If our own journalists have reached such a low point that they're not able to distinguish an Iraqi from a Japanese, then we are worse off than I thought.

I had the archaeologists from the seminar over for dinner, a good party. All their dig houses have been burned or pillaged for building materials and whatever was inside. Iraq does not have the money to pay for site guards. Anyway, what can one pathetic guard do against a gang intent on destruction? Foreign archaeological missions are not allowed to come and excavate – part of the cultural embargo and boycott. Only the Italians have managed to get round that ban. They are digging in Hatra and calling it research.

14 December
The newspapers are now 30 centimetres long and 20 wide, with tiny print. They're economizing on paper, and a good thing too.

(I keep seeing stacks of wasted *New York Times* on the streets of that city.) Our papers are a joke but I approve of their looks. Went to pick up a letter from Lubna, and Mahmood showed me our new stamps. The government is printing five or six dinars on old stamps – reuse of materials. Najul says if we're still in the same situation this time next year, we'll have to unravel our old socks and reknit them. They are already beginning to have holes.

Jabra* has died of a heart attack. That is the end of a cultural era. What a year this has been. I wish it could end sooner. It's making me very nervous. I never got to talk to him this time. Every time I said I would invite him for dinner, I couldn't figure out who could drive him to the house. Even Fakhri had given up driving. It is a great loss.

Salvi has started chasing the ladies again. He disappeared for three days and came back this morning looking completely knackered. He's gone again tonight, leaving two sons on his blanket as replacements.

15 December

We have another mouse/rat in the studio. It too ate through two days of poisoned sandwiches, but it is still around and shitting. Today I found that it had taken the packet of poison seeds to a hiding place. Obviously he/she likes the stuff. So I went to a pharmacist friend and asked for a stronger poison. 'The shelves are all empty,' she said. She now opens for two hours a day. No point when there's nothing to sell. She told me her rat story. She had put down poison, knowing there was a rat somewhere, and then a smell started coming from behind her shelves, so she pulled them from the wall and in a space between, she found half-eaten bars of soap and tubes of medicine that had been sucked dry. Apparently rats love to eat cortisone pills. Maybe my poison is out of date.

---

*   Jabra Ibrahim Jabra: famous Iraqi author and literary figure.

The UN has found that we were hiding something else – a Chinese radar installation and chemical germ warfare stuff, seven tons of which seem to be missing. Sanctions will continue.

16 December

We planted nearly a kilo of onion seeds today. We had so many that I planted them even among the roses and sweet peas. It will be interesting to see whether an onion smell will permeate the roses, or vice versa. Sol might be coming tonight. I'm off to see Naila, who had a horror adventure the other day. She was driving her car and had stopped at traffic lights when a man opened the side door, got in, said 'hello', and proceeded to shove and push her out of the car. Since she is large and he was small, they had a good tussle. He punched her in the eye; she grabbed him by the throat. They struggled and he ended up running away. All this on a main street at seven in the evening. She now has half a black eye. Her cousin asked her whether the guy was trying to steal the car or making a pass at her.

17 December

Sol phoned at four in the morning. I dressed and rushed out in the car to go and fetch her. No Salvi, but once on the road, Salvi, Blackie and three generations of sons started chasing after the car and barking. I tried to talk sense to Salvi but couldn't get through. I was worried that he'd continue to follow me so I returned to the house with the whole pack of dogs behind me. I opened the gates and as Salvi rushed in, I shut the gate behind him – he was looking foolish and shifty. The others chased me for a block and then gave up. I locked myself into the car after Naila's story. One can't be too careful these days. Arrived at the Rashid Hotel to see Sol and Lamia standing outside like two Orphan Annies, baggage piled up around them – all Sol's because Lamia was staying at the hotel. Arrived back at the house. Salvi was at the gate, looking cross. I opened the gate and he went out into the night to join his extended family – gave me a dirty look on the way.

24 December

The other day in the *souq* I saw pullovers manufactured in Iraq on show in a shop window, multi-coloured with little black and white pandas on them, and right across the front the letters BANDA written in English – all colours. I took Sol to see them today, but there were only a few left. Obviously a popular line. Found other spelling mistakes on pullovers. A few had WIMTER, and one had BUEERELY written on it, and was surrounded by flying butterflies. Someone in this factory should be taught to spell.

25 December

Ate a lot of food at lunch today at Assia's. She was running a high temperature from the flu. They killed their poor old turkey, stuffed it and sat it on a bed of rice. She told me that the day before, when she went out to kill the turkey, it thought it was going to be fed – it gave her a very pained look as she killed it.

'Poor turkey', I said.

'We didn't want to eat it,' she said, 'but we have to have a bird for Christmas, and anyway, she hasn't been laying eggs for two months.' Needless to say, none of us ate that miserable turkey – Salvi got the bones. He has two drawers full of bones in my freezer. The UNESCO representative was also at the lunch and said that in prior years his friends would drop by for drinks but now no one comes. They cannot afford to return his hospitality. He has been in Baghdad for four years, so he can see the difference.

My tyres were getting flat so on the way home I went to put air in them. The garage attendant asked why I'd let them get so low. I said, 'Because I've been ferrying a car full of women.'

'Tell them to go on a diet,' he replied, with a huge laugh.

The telephone lines are frozen. One spends one's time yelling 'hello' and not getting anywhere.

26 December

I've been noticing something that one would never have seen before the embargo: middle-class people, not badly off, their sheer nylon stockings showing little mends. I have given four of my tights to Ma to darn, not sheer ones but the thick, coloured, woollen ones. The nicest thing about winter is that one can have coloured legs.

Ma went today to Ghassan's funeral. She said that by the time they'd butchered the sheep, half of it had already been stolen! Sacks of flour and sugar were being pilfered – nothing is sacred any more. Everyone has to bring foodstuffs to funerals to help out the bereaved family. In these hard times nobody can afford to feed the visitors who come to pay their respects, or even to feed the poor as one is supposed to.

3 January 1995 – Baghdad

Lunch at Salima's. Loma was telling me about her university classes; she teaches computer studies. She has sixty students. They have no paper and no pencils. They write on the backs of receipts, pharmacy bills, account books, anything that has a blank side to it. The university does not supply her with paper to photocopy the exams, so she has to write the exam on the blackboard; those at the back cannot see it so when the ones in front have copied the questions, those at the back move to the front. There are only ten working computers, so they take turns on the machines. Some students even do alternate years at the university as their parents cannot afford to pay for their studies. They work for a year and then come back to study for a year – a lot of them fail on purpose so that they don't have to go into the army.

6 January

At dinner tonight, Suha told us of a conversation overheard by a friend at a wedding. They were standing in line at the buffet table, which had a whole lot of cats lurking underneath it. 'Piss off, cats,' the lady in front of her said. 'There's hardly any meat for us, let alone bones for you.' Assia told me that her chickens have taken to committing suicide by throwing themselves into the swimming pool. The first drowned chicken was thrown into the river, the second likewise. Then Assia thought of cooking these chickens for the dog, so as the third drowned chicken was being cooked, her mother walked in and said, 'No wonder you've been sick these past few days, if you've been eating chicken not killed by *halal*.'* Assia told her that it was for the dog and that he's not a Muslim – but her mother wasn't convinced.

13 January

For the first time, Friday the 13th has brought me bad luck. Just opened the boot of the car to remove some bones for Salvi (a present from Tawadud), to find my two empty beer crates, the spare tyre and the jack gone. The thieves obviously don't have a dog, otherwise they would have taken Salvi's bones too. On the other hand, I was lucky they didn't steal the car. Good thing I had the steering lock. Maybe I wasn't so unlucky after all. Story going around Baghdad about two women who were kidnapped, raped, ransomed, burnt with cigarette butts and then dumped naked but alive. They are both semi-crazed and in hospital.

The embargo has been renewed.

14 January

Abu Ali is going to take me to the thieves' market on Friday to buy a spare tyre. There's no point in buying a new one in case

---

* Killed in accordance with Muslim law.

of another theft. Sol and I went and had a picnic lunch in Sippar with Munir and Ismail. The guard dogs are skin and bones, even though they bring them bones every time they come out to the site. Their dig budget is virtually non-existent. There's not enough money to pay for the guards and dog food.

15 January

I found my dentist, what a relief. I've had two filling emergencies on the same tooth; the first fell out in two days, the second gave me swollen gums and also fell out. I wonder if the materials were out of date. Amal could not find her proper dentist (telephones being what they are) and had to go to a dentist who was a relative. He smashed her teeth up so badly that one got loose and she was frightened of swallowing it at night. She has now found, and returned to, her original dentist.

Ma and Needles' telephone has been out of order. Needles said that the telephone wire was lying out in the street. They finally had it repaired and now they seem to have a joint line with an Umm Hussein who talks the whole time. There is also an added crackle and buzz.

Suha has bars on all the windows of her workshop, and when she went there today she found that the whole electricity board had been stolen – the only thing outside the shop! Ahmed (who works in the same building) was with patients when his electricity went out, so he lit candles, being well prepared. Later, when he went to check, he found that the fuses of the entire building had been stolen. They are very expensive to buy, but so easy to lift.

There is talk of medals being handed out on 17 January for the celebrations of Army Day. How can we get everything so ass-backwards? Ma said, 'like camel's pee', which apparently does go backwards. I remember an article many years ago that described Yemen as charging full speed ahead from the fourteenth into the twentieth century. We are doing exactly the opposite. I'm so depressed these days, in the depths of gloom and despair, even my beloved palm trees seem lifeless. Poor Sol came all cheerful and full of strength but by the time she left, all her energy had been drained.

18 January

Went to my dentist. He told me that in the old days he would charge 20 dinars for a filling, his actual costs came to 4 dinars and he would pocket 16 dinars. With that he could buy five chickens. Now a filling costs 1,250 dinars and his profit is 400 dinars, which would just buy him a chicken leg. He cannot afford to travel anywhere. Doctors and engineers have to pay a million-dinar guarantee to ensure their return; some mortgage their houses to get permission to leave.

Salvi has disappeared; now Blackie sleeps on his blanket. Abu Ali said that Salvi came back at noon, wagged his tail, saw I wasn't there and went off again.

19 January

Assia and I have decided to import donkeys from Yemen – there are hundreds of donkeys out of work in the Hadhramawt, all waiting for a job. I saw them there last year. According to Assia, all our cars will be incapacitated and beyond repair in a few years' time – the assumption being that the embargo will not be lifted for some years (our Tarot card readings don't agree with that). We will then be car-less, and bikes and donkeys will be the ideal and popular solution. So we had better start importing them now before donkey prices soar. We are importing second-hand tyres from Jordan; they're already worn down by the time they get here. Few people have spares, and one frequently sees cars propped up on bricks while they go off to repair the punctured tyre. They come back to find more parts missing from their cars.

21 January

A Dutch producer phoned me today; he had read my Baghdad diaries, phoned Sol and told her he wanted to make a documentary on Iraqi artists. 'Are you working on any art?' he asked me.

I said, 'I barely have time, between mending my car, fixing my teeth, repairing the loo and generally rushing around like a headless chicken.' He seemed interested anyway. It would be fun and a change.

Salvi has been away for two days; Majeed has seen him and fed him. Today I saw him – great rejoicing on his part even though he was limping from a thorn in his foot. He ate his food and rushed off to some dog corner in the orchard where they're all having an orgy. The bloody guys mending the water tank for the Italians who are renting Dood's house have drained all the water out, even after I told them that the tanks of the two houses were connected. Stupid twits. I was in the shower covered with soap when the taps ran dry, first the hot and then the cold. I came out frozen solid.

25 January

Hamdiya said to me in a coy way, 'I asked Majeed, why don't you beat me?'

I said, 'Are you crazy? Why do you want him to beat you?'

She said, 'He's cross with me now and won't speak to me because I asked him that question. All my sisters-in-law get beaten by their husbands.' She then added, 'But I was only joking. If he beat me I would commit suicide.' She has a funny way of flirting with that poor husband of hers.

John Lancaster, a correspondent with the *Washington Post*, came to dinner. I've never met him before. I said, 'Would you like to meet a bunch of women?'

'Absolutely,' he said. So we had Ma and Needles, Amal, Suha, Assia and myself – six women in all. I must say, he did quite well. He got an earful. 'Good for me,' he said.

The major topic of conversation was whether Iraq could be divided. We all agreed on the following: that Iraq is situated at a crossroads, that all Iraqis are of mixed blood – Kurdish, Turkish, Persian – and of different religions – Sunna and Shi'a, Christians and Yezidis – and that this diverse group has been living fairly amicably together for centuries. How can they now divide us?

26 January

A mended typewriter. Salvi off again for two days. Abu Ali, from his vantage point mending the roof, saw five different groups of dogs running around yesterday – some party they must be having. It's a relief not to have him around while doing building repairs. He would not have allowed anyone to function properly. While Salvi is out enjoying his dog life, 90 percent of the human population of Iraq are ill with some kind of flu, fever or allergy. Our paranoia is so strong that we all believe that a bug has been introduced into our environment by the USA. We don't believe in natural viruses or flu epidemics any more. I think that all Iraqis suffer from Gulf War Syndrome.

We've had no electricity since 5 p.m. yesterday afternoon, the fault not from the house but from the street. When the maintenance people came, they stood outside the gate and said, 'Where's the dog?'

'Why?' I asked, 'do you know him?'

'Do we know him?' they replied. 'If he's here we're not coming in.' That Salvi has some reputation. I assured them of his absence.

I forgot to pass on to Sol my latest medicinal advice for Doc Q when she phoned last night. Apparently the steam from boiling turnips helps asthma sufferers breathe better – we are experimenting with Umm Raad, who has bad asthma.

Terrible rumours circulating around Baghdad about the ultimate fate of the people involved in the recent attempted coup. Their leader was apparently tied to a horse and dragged around the parade grounds; the others were thrown to starving dogs, trained to maul.

One sees the strangest people begging these days – embarrassed hands stretched out by very respectable-looking people – one knows they must be desperate. They can't make ends meet, no matter how hard they work; salaries are so low.

27 January
Kiko phoned at seven in the morning to wish me a happy birthday. We had a super long conversation, that made my day. I told him that we were going to Suha's house in the country – a pack of women instead of a pack of dogs, with a few token straggler chaps. Sure enough, a few bods and an Eric from Austria showed up – very diplomatic and polite to the ladies, with a special word for each one.

For the third day no Salvi. Everyone feeling a bit sick. Is there something in the air?

28 January
Salvi came back, battered but jubilant – his leg seems to be busted. I tied him up for a few hours but he howled non-stop, his eyes longingly on the orchard. Finally I turned him loose and he rushed off in a hobble.

Every day someone else's house is robbed. Ma insists that I put bars on my kitchen doors, which are just glass. I said, what's the point? They're lifting doors in their entirety.

30 January
Invited to a tea party at the Rashid Hotel. It wasn't what we thought it was going to be – a diplomats' wives charity benefit, whatever that may mean. There were hardly any Iraqis present,

a few from the foreign office, us pack of girls from the Suleikh, Selwa and a whole lot of ambassadors. There wasn't anything for sale, there was some music, a few national dances and booths showing ethnic wares. Met the Pole – quite dapper. Got a lovely belt made from shells from the Philippines stall. Isabel was there – she's still trying to solve the environmental problems of this country by planting trees from different countries. She's working with Hussein Kamel* and thinks he's great – they let her do her thing and she's impressed with that. Why not? Anything that comes for free from the outside world is worth a try as far as the government is concerned.

31 January

John came to say goodbye. He has gone to the brewery and seen that all the vats have been marked for specific use by the UN inspection team, yeast on the yeast vat, etc.

Salvi returned like a soldier broken by the wars, dragging his feet behind him and limping with his front leg. He is filthy, and eats and sleeps not in his usual place but with an eye on any activity by the front gate.

Went with Ferri and Ramzi for the day on their farm outside Baghdad. Ferri spent the war there. She said the missiles would come very low over the farm and then arch and rise to hit their targets. Guided missiles, I said. On the way back we passed by the baby-milk factory that got bombed as a chemical warfare factory – all repaired and working again as a milk factory.

The 250-dinar note was issued and instantly withdrawn from use. It is rumoured that a whole pile of them were stolen and the only way to find the thieves is to withdraw them from circulation until the culprits are caught. If anyone gives you a 250 note, refuse to take it, say the rumour mills. I should think

---

*   Lieutenant-General Hussein Kamel al-Majid: son-in-law of Saddam Hussein and the former head of Iraq's secret military programmes – *see below*.

that the government is just scared that prices will skyrocket even more. The *dinar* will reach 1,000 to the dollar, I'm sure of it. (In January 1996 the *dinar* rose to 3,000 to the dollar, then settled at under 1,000.)

Our Muhammad has been going to the dentistry school to be fitted with a new set of false teeth. One set is free on the government if you allow students of dentistry to practise on you. For the last three weeks he has been going there; they look into his mouth, take a cast, fiddle about and say come back next week. Yesterday he came back with a new set of teeth in place. They look like a great pile of white tombstones. Every time he opens his mouth they get in the way. He said it will take a lot of getting used to.

4 February

That is what my lovely David Hockney calendar says. Mount Fuji with flowers. My telephone is out of order again. I am totally isolated in my ivory tower, though I could talk to my typewriter. I'm cooking dinner for a party tomorrow. Yesterday evening we went to the Alwiyah Club and heard a talk given by Dr Kamal Samara'i, the first Iraqi gynaecologist. During question time a man asked him how he had coped with the conservatism of women, and how he had given them check-ups. His answer was that some would pick up their *abbas** and flee at the very mention of a physical examination. Those who stayed were told it would be half-price. Some accepted the bargain, saying their fate was now in God's hands; others would ask for a divorce after the examination, saying that otherwise he could not have given them a check-up. Did they think that they became the property of the man who touched them? Very odd.

While he was an intern, my great-uncle Sa'ib was the chief surgeon and head of that hospital. The day that King Ghazi died, he was called on to check the body for the death

---

*   Long, all-enveloping, cloak-like garments.

certificate. He confided to Dr Kamal that he did not think that the hit on the head was in the right place for the way the king's car had crashed into the pole. He was sure that the British were responsible for his death. Ma also got up and said that her uncle had told her the same story and that he was convinced it was not a natural crash or a suicide; he had not wanted to sign the death certificate at all. She also thanked Dr Kamal for saving her life after she had delivered Dood. She had such a high temperature that she was burning up and dying; he packed her in ice and she recovered. Some fever!

11 February
Medhat had to go and have a hernia operation at the government nursing hospital. He arrived and was put on a filthy dirty sponge mattress. 'You have to bring your own sheets,' said the nurse.

The heater was dead in his freezing cold room. 'We don't have spare parts to mend it,' said the nurse, 'you have to bring your own.' There were no bulbs in the light fixtures. 'The patients take them,' said the nurse, 'you have to bring your own.' At lunchtime a large nurse comes round the ward swinging a big ladle in her hand. 'Where's your plate?' she asked poor old Medhat. 'You have to provide your own.'

'Why don't you tell us all this before we come in so that we come supplied?' asked Medhat (who loves eating). 'Do you mean to say that I won't get anything to eat now?'

'Well,' she said, 'this time I'll give you your lunch on a tray.' They get boiled rice with a bit of tomato sauce mixed with a few chickpeas, and for dinner boiled rice soup – so much for service in a two-person suite. That night his room companion got terrible cramps (something was wrong with his blood circulation) and he began ranting and raving, so Medhat had to go and search for a doctor. After much wandering he found a nurse who told him that there was no doctor on night duty – only the main hospital ten minutes' walk away had a doctor in attendance. She added that no one would come out on such a freezing night as this. 'Tell him to stand up on his feet and get the blood going, walk him a bit,' she said.

'He can't,' answered Medhat.

'Well, he'll just have to wait 'til the morning,' she replied.

'He could die,' said Medhat. She shrugged her shoulders.

All the handles on the loo doors had been stolen – round, empty holes face you when you sit on the toilet. The man got better soon, and left after two days to recuperate at home.

Medhat also told us stories about his false teeth. The first lot made a whistling noise and were so loose that they would shoot out of his mouth if he talked too fast. He took them back for a check-up. 'They're not loose,' the dentist said, as he put them back in and patted Medhat's cheeks, 'just close your mouth and then open it.' They promptly fell out. 'Well,' he said, 'you've lost weight.' He made him a second pair which broke in the middle within two weeks.

'That's simple,' the dentist said, 'we'll just mend them.'

'What's the point?' asked Medhat, 'if the new ones broke in two weeks?' They glued them together and in a couple of days they came apart in exactly the same place. They made him another set but he never wears them. He went to another dentist, who asked him whether he had difficulty eating without his top teeth in. 'No,' said Medhat.

'OK,' answered the dentist, 'just eat without them. Nothing can replace the teeth that God gave you.' So Medhat now eats only with his lower teeth and all seems well; the new ones are kept in reserve. Our Muhammad takes his new set of shining white teeth out when he eats.

'What's the point,' I asked, 'when they're supposed to help you eat?'

'No,' said Muhammad, 'I bash myself with them and I can't chew when I have them in.'

12 February
Went to the Rashid Hotel to give a letter to Appolone to post, and saw Isabel. She was on the verge of a nervous breakdown – she has no clothing choices left, only two dresses and the jeans she was wearing. Apparently there is a well-known mafia of hotel staff members who rob the guests. When she comes to Iraq with medicines to distribute she immediately calls the parties concerned, but in the time that it takes her to go down to pick them up from the lobby and take them up to her room, all the medicines have disappeared. She says they listen in on telephone conversations and act immediately. She has learned not to say anything on the telephone. Appolone agreed with her. When he arrives at the Rashid, he calls the staff responsible for his room, lays out everything on the bed and tells them, 'I have so many shirts, trousers, socks, etc and would like to keep that many.' He then gives them all a tip and manages to survive his stay relatively intact.

13 February
I got a cordless telephone installed in my house yesterday and this morning I proudly walked about with it in my studio. It never stopped ringing. I would pick it up and it would stop or go off. Rushdie said someone nearby must have a similar one. By 1.30 I was going bonkers with this thing ringing off and on all the time, and I gave up on it. I handed it over to Rushdie who will try it out in his house and see how it works there. Other people have cordless telephones that don't behave that way. Why not me?

I walked with Amal in the *souq*, down the new riverfront. Found a lovely silver box as a present for Dood. On one side it has a map of Bahrain showing the air route to Baghdad, and on the other the route to Karachi with pearl-fishing scenes carved on it. Just beautiful. I bought myself a Sassanian seal with a lovely fellow on it with a wonderfully ornate hairdo. I couldn't resist adding him to the two others that I wear around my neck.

I am past chap time, I think, although one never gives up hope. I certainly look haggard enough.

Went to visit Tawadud in the evening, taking my usual present for her from Salvi – a bunch of violets. She's a super person, somewhere between eighty and ninety years old, deaf as a post, quite ill but always laughing and cheerful in the face of misery. Qusay, her son, has just had an operation to check on his lymph nodes; the prognosis does not look good. His doctor told him that he's been seeing many such lumps since the war; he thinks it's connected with the after-effects of the bombing.

They have upped the exit tax to 100,000 dinars.

14 February

I am in a frenzy of artistic activity and feel more cheerful. I hope it continues. Munir came and paid me for the kilns. He says that the palace wants to use them as pizza ovens! I told him they can't be used for that purpose, those kilns go up to 1,300 degrees! They'll only use them up to 500 degrees, he said. No wonder we go backwards in this country. Such ignorance.

Said is redoing their old *khan* with cement. Horrible. I met the man who pays for his rent in eggs. He was busy replastering the walls of his shop and patching up the ceilings with cement, even though one could see huge holes where termites had been busy. I said to him, 'Don't you see that your ceiling is all rotten?'

'I'm going to prop it up with these iron rods,' he answered. I hope he doesn't keep his eggs there. The whole *khan* is riddled with termites – Said is giving me two old wooden columns that have termites. There were some very strange-looking light bulbs in his office – large and made of blown glass with the Shabandar name written on them.

'What are they?' I asked.

'They're between 80 and 100 years old,' he said, 'ordered by my grandfather, and they still work.' The bottom fixture was busted but he will fit on new ones and reuse them. He is interested in old fixtures so will look after them, but is totally uninterested in old buildings and is doing a really bad job of remodelling the *khan*.

Suhair says a lot of sixteen- to eighteen-year-olds are being brought into hospital with fainting spells or in a coma, and they then die in two or three days. Another after-effect of the war?

We were shown an extraordinary film on TV about two guys who killed an entire family. The whole crime was re-enacted in the house, and was followed by the trial in which both were convicted. They will hang. Hundreds are killed every day. What's so special about this case? Suhair said they were security types and they have to make a show of them.

16 February
There's a terrible fight going on in the orchard between a couple of magpies. Other magpies flew in to watch – even a crow. The din stops and we have a bit of quiet, then he turns up again (I presume it's a he), and the whole racket starts over. Great flapping of wings and flying between palm fronds, maybe it's an extramarital affair and the husband has found out. I wonder if that kind of thing goes on with birds?

I'm in love with Arthur Danto. If there was one reason for me to go to the USA it would be to meet him. He's at Columbia University, so I must tell Sol to find him. On the whole, I hate art critics; they are pretentious and say nothing, but he is wondrous, a revelation, and writes humour. What more could one want? I've not been able to work in months and he inspired me to work again.

My heart feels very heavy because Tawadud is not well and Qusay looks like a goner – that means she won't survive long after him. We went and visited them again and although the results are not out, they seem better. Ma took her one of her cakes and Needles unknowingly put her foot in it (it was on the floor of the car in a plastic bag). Ma sort of patted it into shape again.

No Salvi for two days now, but the horrific dog barking starts about 2 a.m. and continues until five in the morning; total pandemonium in the orchard.

17 February

Maysa, Suhair's daughter, said there's too much talk these days about Gulf War Syndrome. Everyone has that, it's the norm now in Baghdad. But we're dealing with basic diseases like cholera, polio, TB, major stuff, she continued. Gulf War Syndrome talk is for those who don't know what's happening in the hospitals. Gynaecologists are reusing disposable gloves, just dipping them in Dettol, same with disposable syringes. The anaesthetic that is used has come as gifts from various countries, different brands, and no one knows the strengths or what dosage to give to patients – one woman took fifteen hours to wake up from an anaesthetic injection after a Caesarean operation. Surgical thread is some old-fashioned stuff from Pakistan that takes five to eight months to dissolve and causes infections and complications. Anyone over fifty years old is told that there are no medicines; doctors want to keep what little there is for younger patients. That's the level we've reached. I asked her what has really increased since the war.

'Depression,' she answered, 'more than anything else.'

'What do you give them?' I asked.

'Electric shocks,' she said. 'It's faster, leaves no after-effects and is available.' Everyone who was present reacted with ooh ... aah ... how awful, horrible, etc. 'No,' she said, 'it's only Egyptian movies that have made out that electric shock treatment is evil and only for loonies.'

'What percentage of them are women?' I asked. 'Are there more than men?'

'Far more,' she answered. 'They carry all the responsibilities of caring for their house and children on virtually nothing while the men disappear or stay home and sleep.'

There's a story circulating around Baghdad about a father who couldn't support his family any longer; he bought a big fish in the market, poisoned it, and fed it to his family – they all died together. A caring father?

Returned from Hamza with a little carpet for our house in Beirut, very bright colours. Dood called from Abu Dhabi. Apparently Hammoodi is taking religion classes and when Ma asked him how he's doing with the *bismilla*,* he said, 'Oh, we've already passed that!' Our Muhammad was going round the house wearing his cat apron. I told him that his teeth looked better and he said, 'Yes, I'm doctoring them where it hurts. I just file them down.'

'With what?' I asked.

'Anything,' he answered, 'any stone will do. I watched them grinding down my teeth and I too have become a dentist!' They certainly look as if they fit better – he must have been filing them for ages.

Latest gossip is that all Ba'th party** members have to go through religious training; special courses have been set up for them. Will they make the women wrap up their heads in those horrible scarves, like bandages?

20 February

While Ma was at the oculist yesterday, a nicely dressed man came into the shop and asked if he could sell his glasses – tragic and pathetic. Went and visited Hajir in the evening, she lives in an isolated bit of the old world. The walls tell their own story – kings, queens and princes, most of them dead. She has a

---

*   'In the name of God, the Merciful, the Compassionate.'

**   The ruling party in Iraq.

wonderful photo of King Faisal[*] aged about seven, standing with Queen Alia[**] and King Ghazi. He looks so innocent and pure, a shining picture. Ma said, 'Hajir, you know who's missing from your walls?' No comment on that one of course. She won't even leave the country because it will mean that she has to travel holding their passport and she has vowed not to do so as long as they're in power.

21 February
Davies phoned from London – she saw us all on TV, just by chance. She said we were all very good and then she cried. Christina also phoned, so I said, 'Did you see the TV programme?'

'No,' she said, 'I just wanted to know how you were all coping.' That was very touching; she is a strange and mysterious creature. Menth also phoned; Needles was thrilled. My new Korean (Supra) cordless telephone is now installed upstairs. It hasn't rung yet, unlike the other one, which never stopped ringing.

Salvi is stuck to his black lady friend. He's terribly in love, and fiercely guards her from others who fancy her. When I last saw Salvi and his lady, they were lying on the grass while three other dogs on the wall and two in a ditch eyed them jealously. Salvi was looking utterly haggard. He hasn't come to eat for three days.

24 February
I have befriended a robin. I looked him up in my bird book, just to double-check because I didn't expect to find a robin here. He likes dates, therefore he must be an Iraqi robin. He lives in the bougainvillea by my studio and chirps non-stop. If I don't go out and see him every now and then he will not stop chirping,

---

[*]   King Faisal II, king of Iraq, 1935–1958.
[**]   Wife of King Ghazi of Iraq.

but when I do he shows off, leaping and flying and looking to see whether I'm watching. I hope I can train him to come and visit me in my studio; he seems to be on his own, which is strange.

Saw Hashim and he told me that all party members have been asked to pray publicly in the parade ground. I told him that they would put scarves on their heads too if he didn't watch out. He laughed nervously and said, 'No, only on the women.' Meanwhile, Albright is going on a tour of France and Russia to convince those powers not to talk about lifting the sanctions against us. My favourite cartoon now is in my *Guardian Weekly*: it shows US soldiers arriving in Haiti and being greeted by a whole bunch of natives waving banners and yelling, 'Hello dim or crazy' or 'dumb and crazy' and 'doom or crazy', and one soldier with a very pained expression on his face saying, 'It's democracy!' It's by KAL from the *Baltimore Sun*.

Suha and Assia came by. Assia was very funny, telling us about a friend of hers who now has red hair. 'What happened?' asked Assia.

'I can't afford my hair dye,' she said, 'so I'm using vinegar.' Her mother apparently now puts eggplant skin on her hair! Assia is now washing her hair with Tide, she can't afford shampoo and says it makes better suds anyway. She has almost shaved her head so she only has to go to a hairdresser once every four months. I told her I would cut it for nothing. I've been doing mine for the last thirty years. She took her father to the hairdresser and had his hair shaved off too. Assia says that over the years she must have donated over 20 pints of blood for the Palestinian cause; she will not do so again because everyone has ratted on us – it's difficult to get one's blood back. She's also having difficulties with her teeth – a new bridge that makes chewing and talking tricky.

25 February
The orchard is full of white butterflies and fighting magpies. One group is very silent, the other really noisy. Salvi has found someone new, a fawn-coloured dog that looks like one of his babies. They are both parked on the wall. A whole pile of dogs looks on.

26 February
I feel as if I'm living on an animal farm. While I was on the phone I heard a clinking sound coming from near my vegetable rack, so I went to take a look and there was a long tail sticking out of a bag of wheat – a palm-tree rat chomping away and not at all bothered by my yelling. I screamed for Majeed, who came running. The rat continued to eat – it only ran out the door when Majeed grabbed a rag and began to hit him. 'Are they deaf?' I asked Leila when she passed by later in the day.

'No, just hungry,' she answered, 'hungry like everyone else.' I keep forgetting to shut my kitchen door, which is how all these animals come in. Once a snake tried to get in. It kept throwing itself against the glass door that leads into the kitchen. Much as I love snakes, I didn't fancy having one inside, so I told it so and it slithered away.

Salvi has lost his flea collar. He looks quite deranged. I fed him and he ate a little, all the time looking longingly at his new friend sitting on the wall. When he'd finished, he sauntered past Blackie, peed near her and went to his new friend.

Apparently we returned 30 kilos of uranium to the Russians in part payment for our debt. It had been hidden in a cement bunker, imagine if that had received a direct hit! Got a letter from Freako saying that I had to come to Amman in person to renew my residence permit. What a waste of time – she forgot to send my passport back so I can't even leave. I've decided that I will not go where we're not wanted. I shall remain here with my Iraqi passport until things get better and if they don't improve, then I shall live here in my little paradise and grow old, and probably gaga too.

Rumour has it that a new law states that if one goes through a red light one gets beaten up and put into jail for a week!

1 March

Sol phoned this morning and I took it in bed on my new cordless. I love it. Yesterday Daphne called and I sat and talked to her under the palm trees so that she could get the feel of it. Sometimes I don't work it correctly and it switches off. My passport arrived from Amman. Salvi is back, bedraggled and cut up all over. He is again sleeping peacefully on his blanket after more than a month.

2 March

Everyone is talking about the UN delivering rations to the masses. Ma insists that there is a ship in Basra full of apples and bananas. By the time they sort out the distribution, the bananas will have rotted. Those who receive UN rations will have their Iraqi rations cut, or so say the rumours. Zuhair came today and said that France, the UK and the USA will distribute the rations. Twenty-one items per person, including cans and chocolate. No one knows anything. I think it's all talk, like the endless talk about prices and the cost of everything – it's driving me crazy.

I'm selling everything I don't need from my ceramic days and spending the money as quickly as it comes in. I buy truffles or anything else that I want. There's no point in keeping the money, valueless, photocopied stuff. Who wants to live with a bank full of money and not eat truffles while the season lasts?

Abu Muhsin tells Umm Raad to cook a watery vegetable stew because Adiba doesn't like it that way. He tells Adiba to eat dates and bread, and that the food is for him alone. He has millions in the bank, is ill and is likely to pop off any minute, but he'll hang in there until he sees Adiba into her grave. He's in no hurry to face his enemies when he goes. Every time I see

Adiba, she tells me that I was clever not to have married. She rushed off to put in her false teeth before she told us our fortune in the coffee cups. I have victory and a sword. I told them about a crazy dream I had the other night: I threw myself off a ten- or twelve-storey building because it was the only way I could get down. I wasn't afraid and it was fun. All the people below were yelling, 'You're going to die,' and they tried to catch me so that I wouldn't fall hard on the ground, but I fell softly and all was fine. Since I'm wearing my third chap on a seal, I dream every night like crazy – I put the stone under my pillow and dream away. I think he's Parthian, but he may be Sassanian – lovely hairstyle and beard.

Apparently all out-of-season vegetables on sale in the markets come from the greenhouses of our ruling family; the entire ministry of agriculture is working for them. They also have a gazelle farm and eat gazelle meat.

M.A.W. is back in town. I told him he just missed the dog party that we've been having. He has an air gun that he intends to fire at the dogs when they bother him; the pellets are little pinpricks, he said. But they won't bother him again – the animal lover returned. He was ranting about the state of his garden, saying, 'Look, no grass. Just like a desert with dog holes.' I told him that his gardener Abd had been pinching flowerpots from Suha's house (she has moved to Hisham's in Mansur), that he transplants flowers from M.A.W.'s garden into these pots and sells them. Anyway, I'm glad he's back so that we can play *tric trac** again. He had an awful journey coming back; the driver took seven hours to shit and two hours to pee and five hours to eat! I said, 'You must have been on the road for days!' He's a first-class exaggerator. He came on a new British airline to Beirut that gave out free drinks all the way.

I think I might get a cow. Majeed knows how to milk it, Hamdiya can make yoghurt and we have plenty of greenery to

---

*   Backgammon.

feed it. I thought of goats but they are so destructive and we can't keep them tied up all day. Cows just sort of muck around, and we wouldn't have to buy any more manure for the orchard.

Rolf Ekeus* announced that we had been hiding our germ warfare stuff and not telling them where it was hidden. I can well believe it after hearing the uranium story. The USA has won again, the sanctions will remain. Albright need not have gone on her trip. Everyone in Baghdad calls her Fulbright, I wonder why?

3 March

Just returned from a long day of visitings. Had just finished reading Shirin's book on Princess Fakhrilnissa, badly written but interesting because one knows the people involved. As I was mentally into the Ottoman empire I started on *Regards from a Dead Princess* by Kenizé Mourad, a far more interesting and better written book. Since we still have a few diehard Ottomans left in Baghdad, I went to check on their memories. Ataturk had taken my fancy so I asked Abla Jalila whether she'd ever met him. 'No,'she said. But Nahida, who was visiting her, said that she'd met him twice when she was a student – he was good-looking, with piercing blue eyes. He remembered her when they met again at a function for Reza Shah of Iran, and singled her out. All eyes turned on her, and as she bent to take her first sip of champagne, a great big strawberry hit her and splashed all over the front of her dress. Perturbation all around until the Shah's aide came to her side and said to her, 'In our society, when someone gets too much attention, a fruit is thrown at them to ward off the evil eye,' so everyone relaxed and laughed. Ma said that Ataturk was very friendly with my great-uncle Naji when he was ambassador to Turkey, and later when he

---

*   Chairman of Unscom, the United Nations special commission charged with dismantling Iraq's weapons of mass destruction.

became foreign minister of Iraq – they both liked to drink and flirt, and got along very well.

There was a Swiss epidemiologist at lunch at Assia's and I told him that I hoped epidemics didn't follow him around. He said, 'No. Only work epidemics.' This country is being used as a lab, with all of us as guinea pigs. They're taking count of the last six years and what diseases have increased. He says it's an utter disaster and that they will lift the embargo when they read his report. I told him that this embargo was a political one and would not end until the USA decided to end it. I asked him whether there was an increase in cancer and he said he didn't know, he only does contagious diseases. I told him that he should advise the outside authorities to send a cancer specialist to check whether the pollution of the war (all the chemicals that were thrown at us and that will remain in the soil, acting as a slow poison) has increased that disease. But then I remembered that the USA experimented on its own soldiers, so why should they care if we survive or not? In fact, it's useful for them; they can check the results in total freedom and unhampered by any legal constraints.

I phoned Assia to thank her for lunch and was telling her that I was reading Kenizé Mourad when she said, 'But I knew her well, in the 1970s. She was a journalist for the *Nouvel Observateur* and came often to Baghdad. I would take her round and act as her translator.' Such a small world. Assia says that Kenizé Mourad grew up in an orphanage. How could that be true?

Maybe I should start the family biography that I'm supposed to be writing by listing all the 'firsts' of the family in the early years of the newly independent Iraq. My grandfather founded the Agricultural Bank, my great-uncle Sa'ib was the first surgeon, my father the first agriculturalist/horticulturalist – he began all the experimental farms in Iraq. Even in our generation, Sol was the first woman archaeologist and I was the first woman potter. However, there's no place for us members of the old society in this new one; we don't speak the same language.

A lot of kidnapping is taking place around Baghdad. Here's how it happens: a car stops at the traffic lights, someone points a gun through the window and says, 'Give me your car keys.' While the driver is concentrating on getting the keys, a second person is busy hustling out his woman passenger. She is taken out, raped, beaten, shorn of her hair and finally thrown naked out on the street. The government is apparently worried because they don't know who is responsible for this latest crime wave. It is not limited to a particular area of Baghdad, but happens in different districts.

5 March

God knows what the hell is happening. Turkey has invaded from the north and has supposedly taken Zakho. Iran and the insurgents have invaded the south and the army has been on alert for the last week. Party members are also on alert and manning checkpoints everywhere. Lots of guns have been smuggled into Thawra. Tomatoes have reached 400 dinars a kilo. My tyre mechanic told me today that about six kids between six and seven years old came to him and begged him to give them jobs as they have left school – presumably their families need every bit of extra cash. He himself is an Arabic schoolteacher but is on army duty. He doesn't go to his army job but just gives his salary to his officer – he can't afford to live on the pay with his wife and three kids. The tyres that come into his garage to be repaired have to be seen to be believed. I said, 'Is it possible that a car can even move with tyres worn so smooth that there are chunks missing?'

He just laughed and said, 'This is Iraq the Great. In Kurdistan they call the south "Shi'istan" ("Shi'a-land"), the centre "Ju'istan" ("hunger-land") and the north, naturally, Kurdistan.'

Since M.A.W. returned, the dogs are all back in their place and well behaved, presumably fearing the pellet gun. Salvi has a new follower. I've lost my war with the dogs. I don't have the energy to chase them any more.

6 March

The news does not sound good: Khanaqin has fallen to the Iranians, Zakho to the Kurds and the south gone? (All turned out to be false stories.) Sol phoned from Frankfurt airport on her way to Uzbekistan, lucky thing.

Went to a concert given by a nine-year-old, a little Mozart, truly amazing.

Umm Imad, the maid at Ma and Needles' house, said that if the US army marched into Baghdad they would be welcomed with open arms, adding that if she could smuggle her two boys out of the country she would. It would be worth missing them. Ma calls her the voice of the people, the barometer of Iraq.

8 March

Today the weather is balmy and I'm walking around without socks, a lovely feeling. My friendly robin is still around and demanding breakfast. A pair of nightingales and the magpies have discovered my cache of dates and goodies so there is a lot of activity under the bougainvillea.

Gave a dinner party last night. Excellent. Not only the food but the combination of people – the new Indian ambassador is a poppet. Everyone was doing their own thing, and conversations veered from starving children to epidemics because the Swiss epidemiologist, Dr Bernard, was present. He has fallen in love with Iraq and doesn't want to leave. I gave him Seton Lloyd's book* to photocopy because he wants to learn more about this country. Ala', who only wanted to talk about art, was being pestered by Assia about some weird disease

* *Foundations in the Dust: A Story of Mesopotamian Exploration.*

whose name she couldn't remember, one that eats up the body. 'Can't we forget medicine?' he asked. Dr Bernard and Henry wouldn't stop eating rice so finally Assia went and removed the plate. I made a paté out of Iraqi truffles. Henry said, 'Of course, you *would* get it wrong. In France, truffle paté is presented in minute quantities, while you've done the exact opposite. What extravagance!'

'But these are Iraqi truffles, and I'm happily selling the contents of my studio to buy more,' I said. 'I don't care. One only lives once.'

9 March

I was out in the garden planting tomatoes with Majeed when there was a great clacking noise. 'What's that?' I said. 'Sounds like a duck.'

'No,' said Majeed, 'that's a big snake laying its eggs.' Such a loud noise. I looked closer but couldn't see anything. Presumably they will surface when we clean up the orchard and they have no dead leaves and places to hide under – what an excitement.

10 March

We had a lovely picnic near Salmanpak in an orchard of pear trees belonging to Qahtan. All the trees were in bloom, and it looked like snow on the ground and on the trees, beautiful but no smell. Just the opposite of what I will have in my orchard in a week's time – I will be reeling from the smell of orange blossom. I asked Qahtan whether he'd noticed any difference in his orchard since the war in terms of diseases etc, and he said only odd bugs that he'd never seen before. His gardener brought him what looked like a thick green leaf and as he was scrutinizing and squeezing it, red blood oozed out of it and he realized it was an insect. The gardener plants little shoots and seedlings and they get eaten overnight by strange red worms.

Afterwards, I went to the Rashid Hotel to visit Appolone and saw the ultimate economy that a luxury hotel has to practise during an embargo – in the loo a bar of pink soap had been crudely cut in half, one on each side of the basin. I walked out and ran into Seymour:[*] what's an oil conference without Seymour? He came loaded with goodies for us and also gave me a tape of our BBC interview with Tim.

Found M.A.W. on the road, peeling onions directly into his garbage bin. 'Why don't you do that in your kitchen?' I asked.

'You have to take the onions inside and peel them and bring out the peel again. This is simpler and saves time,' he answered. But I know that the real reason is that he doesn't want to dirty his house. Then he doesn't have to hire anyone to clean it. He's a fetishist about cleanliness.

By my kitchen door there was a bloody kind of worm, I look at it closely and it looks like a queen bee. I asked Majeed whether he'd seen it and he said yes, and that it was about the time when queen bees emerge to make a new hive. That's when the bee-eaters get them. I saw one, a beautiful turquoise with brown and red splashes, drinking water from the swimming pool. He must have been the killer. Poor queen bee, working like a dog all her life, and the minute she comes out for a bit of fresh air she's killed. What a life. Qahtan had 200 beehives but a few years ago they were decimated by an epidemic of red insect-bees that hovered outside the hives and would eat the wings off the bees as they came out -- a veritable disaster that killed off most of the bees in Iraq. That happened just before the Gulf War, so I can't put the blame on the war.

Our new *tanoor* is broken – just bought at terrific expense. Hamdiya and her sisters were carrying it to its site when Salvi came from behind and stuck his nose into Hamdiya's sister's bum. Naturally she screamed and dropped her load. End of *tanoor*.

---

[*]   Editor of *MEES*, an authoritative oil journal published in Cyprus.

15 March

Had dinner last night with Seymour, who told us that the oil conference was a great success, that for the first time the authorities gave them all the documentation they asked for. Dinner went on until 2 a.m. with Ilham playing the guitar. It was fun except that I got very ill from cigarette smoke. It really was killing me. I couldn't breathe and had to take great gulps, my mouth working like that of a fish. I have to give up my smoking friends and just talk to them on the telephone.

Went to mend my car silencer, which has a great big hole in it. It cannot be welded. I have to get another. The man who owns this shop is an ex-civil servant who used to work at the Ministry of Oil, but is now retired. My car mechanic and full-time adviser on cars is an ex-ambassador who retired and opened a mechanic's shop – something his heart had been set on for years. According to his wife Sarab, his holidays were never for relaxation, they were an excuse for stuffing his head into the bowels of a car. He has many people working for him, not your usual car mechanics but sons of friends – more phone every day because there are no jobs around, but he can't take any more. The exhaust man was using his son as a welder.

The situation is getting worse by the minute, but we don't know anything. Lots more dead bodies turning up. They had to clear the hospitals of the not-so-sick to make room for the badly wounded. There's a rumour going round of a failed coup attempt, nipped in the bud.

The other day, all heads of departments and government offices were collected by bus and taken to Tikrit.* All were very nervous, they had no idea what was going to happen to them, but when they arrived at their destination they were given buckets and spades and told to go and collect truffles! They went off happily and collected a sackful to take back home. The

---

*   Town some 160 km north of Baghdad where Saddam Hussein and most members of the Iraqi Ba'thi regime come from.

truffles have been magnificent this year and I'm eating them with everything. Just had them mixed with olive paste and tomatoes – delicious.

They have been trimming the palm trees in the orchard and I got a thorn in my ankle. It was just a little prick but my ankle is now swollen and throbbing in time with the ticking of the clock. Palm thorns are lethal.

Am starting to unpack my summer clothes. Summer will come overnight and I still haven't got the swimming pool in order. The telephone situation is becoming desperate, one screams and yells to a background noise of beeps and drones and crossed or mixed lines. I've just had a screaming match with Ma. When I talked to Seymour, I heard him say he was bringing over three females – in fact he brought over only one. I was just hearing everything wrong.

16 March
Dreamed last night of a two-headed person-cum-donkey – it sort of changed, metamorphosing from one to another: a bad guy stuck to a good guy, making terrible faces. The last thing I was reading last night before I fell asleep was about how, in olden times, Indian princes would cut up two young birds, join them to grow into one, teach them how to fly so they could show their alternating profiles – one side blue feathers, the other pink – sounds grotesque. Then I dreamed of Kruddie and I was so happy to see him that I kept hugging him and talking non-stop. He's been dead for fifteen years and could have told me interesting things: instead I just talked. A missed opportunity – even in dreams.

18 March
Saw Wissam on the news with the Pope – looked in his element with all that wonderful granite and marble at the Vatican. The Pope said the embargo was wrong and only hurt the people, that

embargoes should be used for short and restricted periods only. Tariq Aziz is going to spend the next two months doing an Albright – touring all the countries of the world that will have him. What are we going to offer them, I wonder.

The Red Cross had a luncheon at Amal's Bait al-Iraqi* and she took me along as a token Iraqi. Most were Swiss but there was an Irish lady who's in charge of spare limb parts, fitting them on and teaching the exercises. She says false limbs are the one thing that this country can do, they're cheap to make and not banned under the embargo. There are plenty of people here with missing limbs, and many more every day from exploding landmines. No one has bothered to de-mine the country. Another Red Cross delegate was in charge of missing people, Kuwaitis and Iraqis. I asked her how many and she says about ninety. They've made only one positive identification, a man who came back and didn't bother to inform the Red Cross. When they phoned up his family, he answered and said, 'Oh, I've been back for two years.' They keep the names on their list for nine months. I asked about the Iranians but the Red Cross is not responsible for their count – none of their officials is allowed into Iran. No wonder so many of the Iranian prisoners have not returned or been heard of in years.

29 March
It's been ages since I last wrote. I had a terrible flu and cold, sinus, throat and fever – it still won't go away. I didn't stay a single day in bed but took the latest antibiotic brought by Sol from Q. I'm afraid they didn't do me much good, so went on to Advil, which improved me some. I heard on the BBC today that the USA is the biggest seller of arms. Why don't they make medicines and good things and let the world relax a bit? Enough killing.

---

*   Craft centre, where cultural activities are also held.

Issam came to visit today and raved about the smell of orange blossom. I have gotten used to it. We had a long talk about sewage – he's worried that if there was another attempt made to wipe us out, they might hit the sewage plants instead of the electricity, then we really would be up to our noses in shit. I told him that he should worry about the mess we're in now rather than worry about what may or may not happen – let's first get out of the shit we're now in, metaphorically speaking. Then he started to talk about families, his as against the Gailanis. He can trace his back 200 years while the Gailanis go back to 1120 or thereabouts. But what's the use of that, he says, if no member has shone since Abd al-Qadir,* and that was over 800 years ago; they've all been living off the fame of that one person. Issam is hoping to make something of himself, a bit late in the day but maybe he can solve the sewage problems of Iraq and be remembered forever – he is, after all, a water engineer. My horoscope says my name will live after me, and I must say that we all have not done too badly. Issam says, 'Anyway, you're an *alwiyah* because you come from a *sayid*** family,' but I said that blood must be running a bit thin by now. Must remind him that he forgot about Rashid Ali Gailani.

We laughed a lot but he's very depressed. Until now, he has not had a nice home, the Karrada house is being repaired but there's no water and he makes do with one bucket a day. I took him to my studio to show him my latest madness. I will call this exhibition 'Embargo Art'. All the sculptures, whole families of people made of stone and car parts – busted exhausts and silencers that I collected when I went to mend my silencer – quite funny. The heads are painted stones and come off easily, a recognition of the reality that is present-day Iraq? Issam was

---

*   Abd al-Qadir al-Gailani was a renowned Sufi.

**   Someone who can trace their ancestry back to the Prophet Muhammad.

silent, looking at them, then he said, 'Yes, let's see what people think of them tomorrow at the dinner.'

31 March

I didn't manage to talk to anyone at the party last night because I was so busy and Ma wasn't there to help. Salvi was on the rampage, he nearly bit Alia and did bite Issam. He has forgotten people because he's been chasing his ladies for so long. Now that he's back home, he's taking his guard duties more seriously. I had to tie him up. The black lady is going to have his pups here, I'm sure of that. I try to shoo her away but she won't leave him alone for a second. Issam sat down at the table and didn't stop eating until past midnight. He must store food like a camel, and then not eat until his next invitation. Everyone loved my stone people and they came out of the studio laughing – a good, encouraging reaction. But I don't think anyone will buy this stuff. I have to see what Isabel says about it when she comes tomorrow with Kristoff.* Poor guy, he has to represent US interests here and gets upset by people's reaction to him. He's with the Polish embassy and the Iraqi government asked them to represent the USA; they couldn't say no.

Went to see Hatem and Leila; their antique shop will never get finished, just like my swimming pool. We started discussing the missing chemicals of Iraq and he said that anything was possible, seeing the way ministries were always transferring people around. Files get mislaid. He himself has lost a lot of stuff because he got tired of packing it up and moving it. One can imagine these chemicals buried on someone's farm or property and completely forgotten.

To change the subject, five days ago a yellow lovebird flew in and sat on my window. I called Majeed, who got his ladder and caught her because they cannot live outside. We put her in the cage that belonged to the fancy pigeons that I once kept. I

---

*   The Polish ambassador, representing American interests in Iraq.

used to leave the door of the cage open so the pigeons could fly about, but Salvi was very jealous and would pee on the cage and try to eat them. Anyway, today we took her to the pet shop and got her a mate – a white lovebird – and they immediately began to coo happily to each other. I gave the pair to Majeed and Hamdiya, who are thrilled to have them.

We emptied fifty-five buckets of slimy green water from the swimming pool. We had to do it manually because we don't have a pump and I wanted the pool to dry out. Luckily for us it was not full, now 5 centimetres have emerged in the shallow end.

1 April
Isabel came to visit for the first time, she talked for two and a half hours. I asked her how come the French ambassador was going out with her as I thought she was in their bad books. She said, 'They think I'm sleeping with the president and they have to be friendly!' She also said that the Americans have made a superhighway from Turkey into Zakho in Kurdistan, which is why the army was in there so quickly and efficiently. Her latest suggestion to the Iraqi government is to turn Lake Razzaza into a sanctuary for dolphins – apparently it's the only salt-water lake that is 500 kilometres from the sea. It's large enough, it needs some dredging and planting of seaweed and algae to make it habitable for dolphins. 'A wonderful idea,' I said. 'If you suggested it to the government they might sponsor it.' The only bad thing is that it would become out of bounds for all of us. She loved my 'Embargo Art' and Kristoff said he would do some imaginative publicity about it, something along the lines of how even with an embargo one has not given up. We'll see.

3 April
Am off to meet Kristoff who has found two lovely big car parts and if I like them he'll provide two tough guys to bring them

here. So none other than the US representative is helping me. I'm going to ask him whether he can get a tank to put in front of the Meridien Hotel as part of the embargo exhibition. I will paint it and get everyone I know and people off the streets to write their comments on it. It will be called 'An Anti-Tank Missal'.

4 April

He never showed up. I had gotten so worked up about the whole idea, I feel deflated. I mustn't get so excited about this exhibition. Better tone down my enthusiasm and expectations. I went and saw Ferial to ask about my swimming-pool parts and about a cow. Found a cow but it was too expensive.

I was told that if an embargo is enforced and lasts for over five years, then all debts owed by a country are dismissed. That means that if we survive 'til next year we do not pay our debts. Can that be possible and, if it is, why does no one talk of it? I must check this story for verification.

The BBC says that it will take the USA the whole of the next century to clean up its nuclear waste and at a cost of billions. They will never do it, and will take the world down with them – what an abuse of nature by man.

5 April

All is well again. Kristoff talked to the army and they're thrilled with the idea of my tank. Kristoff asked whether I wouldn't like an aeroplane as well! I laughed and said no, it doesn't have the same meaning for me. Isabel said that while I'm at it I should get more military junk. I asked Medhat whether it's true about a five-year embargo wiping away one's debts. 'No such thing,' he said. 'If it was true we'd be leaping at the chance.' It's only a few more months.

The garden is full of large yellow and black, and orange and black, butterflies.

8 April
One of the men manually pollinating the date palms just fell off one. The palm had been broken and had no head but he was working on automatic, doing them one after the other in a row, and hadn't even noticed that it was dead. It's amazing that he even managed to climb it. Salvi began barking and making a terrible commotion, so I went out but didn't see anything. But Salvi just kept barking, so Hamdiya went and looked and started screaming and yelling that the man was dead in the bushes. He had fallen into a water ditch and couldn't be seen from the house. Hashim came running; he had heard a thump. I only heard Salvi barking and the radio blaring. The poor man turned out to have broken his ankle, so we called his partner and together we bandaged his foot with sticks and a nylon rope and wrapped it in a nylon bag.

11 April
I keep myself sane by making and creating my crazy stone and junky metal bits combinations – art doesn't make sense in this context – this is just junk and funny, helps to lighten up our situation. The exit tariff to travel abroad now costs 200,000 dinars; everyone says that by the summer it will be raised to 500,000.

12 April
The bees have gone crazy for the poppies in the garden. There are about five or six of them per poppy, drinking the nectar – is there opium in it and will the honey carry its effects? I'm typing outside with the butterflies, bees and birds. The garden is beautiful now. Salvi is asleep under the car. Five white butterflies are dancing in front of me. I wonder if those horrid black caterpillars that I killed when I first came could have turned into these beautiful butterflies.

Went to the Indian embassy last night. Other diplomats were envious that the Indian ambassador had managed to gather so many artists at his house. It was a good idea; at the beginning everyone stuck close to those they knew, but after dinner there was much intermingling. Met the Cuban ambassador and wanted to exchange embargo information with him and compare notes – lots of comparisons. He has been posted to the Near East for the last twenty years but doesn't speak any Arabic. He said that at his first posting in Cairo he tried to learn but found the pronunciation difficult and gave up. That doesn't say much for him. His wife is a dyed blonde and they clutched hands throughout the evening – she speaks Spanish and some Russian and was not friendly. He went to get her some dessert and I said but it's the wife who usually does that here, and he said that in Cuba the wife rules and is called 'the Minister of the Interior'. The Yemeni ambassador said that he'd been in Baghdad for six years, and stayed throughout the war. He comes from the northern part of Yemen. Apparently four ambassadors stayed throughout the war – the Russian, Palestinian, Yemeni and the Vatican *nuncio*.

All my solderers (*fitterchiye* in Iraqi dialect, from the English 'fitter') in the garage are out of work. No one has money to repair their cars and so I can't get any more busted parts. They said that they would soon not have money for petrol, and I said, 'Well, that'll mean the end for everyone because it's the only cheap thing left in this country.'

13 April
Just spoke to Amal, her rash is not going away and she's now taking cortisone. It's pouring with rain. She was expecting a visit from the Jordanian ambassador, his wife and many others but had locked herself out of her bedroom and was stuck outside in her nightie with no change of clothes. I told her to wear something of Munir's. He had gone to borrow a tall ladder

from the neighbours so that he could climb in through her window and let her in.

16 April

My exhibition has been moved from 15 to 3 May. I'm in a state of panic. We have not agreed to the UN resolution allowing for a partial lifting of the sanctions. The dollar is going up and down, and with it the price of sugar, rice, etc, etc. People must be making and losing fortunes overnight. Poor Wafa says she's going to pull out six teeth because they all need to have root-canal work and each one would cost 3,000 dinars. It's cheaper just to pull them out. She's as white as a sheet and in constant pain. To think that once upon a time we had a free national health service.

Isabel says that parents are beating up their children because they can then be hospitalized for up to three weeks – there they can be fed.

My beautiful white irises are out, but as soon as a flower comes out, it's covered with little black ants; I wash them with diluted soap and water; five minutes later, other ants take over. Meanwhile, the lovely irises turn a nasty yellow colour – so the lesser of the two evils is to leave them to the ants. Nothing makes sense any more these days.

17 April

I have just been told that one of my three male palm trees is a dud, the one that looks the healthiest. Might as well remove it, said Abu Nizar. Imagine: even palm trees produce beautiful studs that are no good – their pollen is sterile.

This afternoon I'm going to a Harley-Davidson garage. Isabel is mad about them and she thought I might be able to find some junk there. She has stopped looking for trees and likes pipes instead. Kristoff says he might remove all the silencers from their embassy cars and give them to me; they need replacing. I like the idea of dismantling one's car for the sake of ART.

The BBC says that termites produce methane. That means that Iraq is heavily into methane production as the entire country is riddled with termites. We have so many crosses to bear.

18 April

Kristoff phoned this morning and, in his wonderful classical Arabic, said he had a guy with a pick-up truck who could take me round all the garbage dumps in Baghdad. I hooted with laughter. Wonder what security thought of that conversation.

22 April

Working like a dog, my hands in the most awful state – with all these big pipes and iron pieces, one really gets multi-coloured! My mass destructive weapon is done and I will give it eyes tomorrow. It looks quite lethal. Perhaps I will call it 'Creature of Mass Destruction' – 'Destroyer' for short.

Excellent of Qadhafi to send his plane for the *hajjis** to go to Mecca and even more amazing on the part of the Saudis to let them in. Perhaps they're changing. Am glad that the Oklahoma bombing turned out to be a purely American thing, though even now the BBC continues to say that it resembles the New York bombings. They never let up, do they? Somehow there's always an insinuation of an Arab/Muslim hand in anything bad or evil, that is, if they can't blame it on us completely.

7 May

Too busy with the exhibition to write, too difficult to get back into the rhythm of writing every day. I'm forcing myself to start again. Too much has happened and I seem to have lost the thread of the narrative.

---

*   Muslim pilgrims who make the pilgrimage (*hajj*) to Mecca.

Garbage men from the Mansur area are much in demand. They sell their garbage to the highest bidder because the rich people of this wealthy neighbourhood often throw away perfectly good things that can be fixed and resold for more money. To what level have we sunk?

Assia has a whole lot of new teeth that she takes out when she wants to talk. She said they get in the way. She puts them in at night. Hope she doesn't swallow them.

Salvi has taken to sleeping in the studio. Two days ago he started his womanizing again – it can't be the season again so soon. He greeted me at the gate last night, leaping all over me as if to say you are the absent one, not me. I hadn't seen him for two days and had been leaving his food with Majeed. I gave him a midnight snack and he went off scratching. A *bulbul** has made a nest in a rose bush just below eye level. Three eggs, and all have hatched. I'm watching them grow every day. All three are fine.

9 May

Ghazi came yesterday and thought it might be fun if I gave the Destroyer to the Rashid Hotel, where it could be seen by foreigners and Rolf Ekeus too (he should be here by the end of the month). I told him the sculpture had Swedish parts in it – five bits from Amal's Volvo! I asked him about the Bush mosaic at the entrance of the Rashid, apparently it had been commissioned by Uday** and executed by two artists/engineers. The guy in the shop next to Samira's gallery says the Destroyer was made to destroy him. Samira bought up his shop to enlarge her gallery and every night before we close up the exhibition we take in the Destroyer, dragging in a whole pile of sand with it (it sits on a bed of sand). He is taking a long time moving out, this may hasten his departure.

---

*   Nightingale.

**   Eldest son of Saddam Hussein and his wife Sagida.

12 May

The UN is sending in a new group to check our weaponry and chemical stuff. I got into hysterics and phoned up everybody and told them they were coming to check on my Destroyer. I must invite them to the exhibition. Samira said they will either shut down the gallery, and we'll be in trouble, or they will like it. Must take a chance, I said, and she agreed – she's a real sport.

18 May

Dood's birthday and the BBC says it's the Pope's and Margot Fonteyn's too (but she's dead). Had a weird conversation with a sculptor the other day. He is having an exhibition in Jordan and wanted to take out his bronzes for that purpose. He was told that bronze is one of the forbidden materials, reserved for military use only – it cannot leave Iraq. He said, 'Weigh them and I'll bring back double the amount,' but they wouldn't agree. Finally they did agree. Naturally, we were going round imagining how crazy it would be melting down an exhibition, etc, etc.

I came back home for lunch wanting to look up Dadaism because that's what everyone tells me that I'm into. I found an anthology on Picasso that had a small reference to Duchamp, and there on the same page, the story of how Picasso worked in secret during World War II with banned materials (bronze, plaster, etc), materials that were specifically for the use of the Nazis. His friends smuggled them out of factories for him, hiding them under garbage wagons, taking them out right from under the noses of the Nazi guards. So what's new in this world? I learned nothing about Dada.

My vegetable-growing activities have not been too successful. Not one of my million or so onions came out. They just disappeared. My lettuces have grown into trees with blue flowers; the cabbages, cauliflowers, sprouts and broccoli have great big elephant ears and nothing else. The corn shot up and fanlike fronds went on display, so there will be no corn either.

I think my vegetable planting can be termed a failure although the tomatoes are beginning to show. We are waiting for them to turn red. I did get one bunch of runner beans, they were excellent. The greatest struggle was with the dogs, who would lie smack in the middle of the nicely tilled and damp furrows. Majeed had to replant the runner beans umpteen times, the dogs dug everything up. Isabel says that Iraqi runner beans are the best and that we could be growing three crops a year and making a fortune. It's only ten in the morning and the cooler is already blowing out hot air. I guess it's already busted.

19 May
Killed a hunchback cockroach today. If the cockroaches are becoming malformed, what could be happening to us? It had a curved back and looked like a walking arch.

20 May
My mud wall is down. Yesterday I saw it leaning and told Abu Ali to find someone to patch and buttress it. He said he would bring it all down and rebuild it. Well, it's now down, the dogs will love it.

The sculptor has not been given permission to take out his bronzes. He is depressed and wants to leave and not come back. I met another sculptor and gave him a lift home – he was clutching a box that looked like one used to house binoculars, but he said it wasn't. He had taken it off a dead Iranian soldier during the Iran-Iraq war. It had 'Beethoven' written on it and under that it said 'dynamite explosives'. Imagine calling a dynamite box a 'Beethoven' – why? Because he was deaf? I asked him whether they took the name tags of dead soldiers first. 'Nothing doing,' he said. 'Each person does their own thing – those who steal, steal what they like first.' Since he always liked antiques and old things, he spent his time looking at mounds and archaeological sites, but when he came across this box he took it, thinking it might be useful. He said there were so many dead that one got used to it.

When Imad arrived home after being held as a prisoner-of-war in Iran for nine years, the first thing he wanted was a bath – he wallowed for hours in soaps and perfumes. Then came down and wanted a huge breakfast of eggs, sausages, HP sauce, etc, reverting to his early days in the UK. He said being a prisoner hadn't changed him, but I don't believe that. They did all sorts of terrible things to him, including seven months in solitary confinement in a loo – naked with buckets of shit being thrown on him. He taught English when he was not in solitary (in secret as it was not allowed) and whenever he could, day or night, and kept himself sane that way.

Isabel's appointment yesterday with Uday was cancelled after a wait of seven hours. They said they would call her again, and the next day they gave her a 6.30 p.m. rendezvous. The woman who came to pick her up was horrified by her casual outfit and insisted that she put on a smart dress and make-up. Isabel said, 'That's the way I am, take it or leave it.' The woman started to plead with her, saying, 'You have to be nicely dressed.' At that point Isabel refused to go and slammed the door in the lady's face while she was still pleading with her.

The trees are full of young birds learning to fly, they do it in spurts an inch behind their mum or whomever is teaching them.

29 May

Salman Shukr* says that his father broke fourteen of his *ouds*** because he didn't want him to study music. 'You are shaming me in front of my friends,' he told his son.

'But my grandmother used to play the *oud* and it was not considered shameful,' answered Salman.

---

*   Famous Iraqi *oud*-player.

**   Stringed instrument, similar to a lute.

'That's the difference between the Rasafi and the Karkh sides of the river,' said his father. 'There's a lag of a few centuries between the two banks of the river.' Years later, when Salman had become a renowned and internationally famous musician, he asked his father whether he now accepted and enjoyed his success as an *oud*-player. 'No,' said his father, 'now you have shamed me in front of the whole world.'

Embargo talk: chickens are being fed with mouldy bread, a form of natural antibiotic because there are none to give them. Maybe that's the way dogs protect themselves, they eat the rottenest things – all dead and mouldy. Najul says that when she was a child she got bitten by a Baghdad Boil Fly,* and her aunt got some chicken shit and rubbed it on that place and it never took. Must ask Q what he thinks of this bit of medical information. Aspirin is made from eucalyptus bark, just learned that.

Boris and Neal** left this morning – got used to having them around, though I was working so hard on finishing the two portraits I didn't spend as much time as I'd have liked with them. To every question Boris now replies, 'It's the embargo.'

31 May

M.A.W. is on the warpath. I went out this morning to find him standing at the gate with two men, one with a rifle. They said they were from the Ministry of the Interior and had come to shoot dogs because a complaint had been lodged against them. I told M.A.W. that he had better not shoot Salvi or I'd never speak to him again. He was practically frothing at the mouth and yelling, 'I'll shoot "Salvi" *and* you! What sort of neighbour are you, having dogs that ruin my garden!'

---

*   The bite of this sandfly causes a boil that leaves a scar after it has healed.

**   Visiting Dutch musicians.

'You have no garden!' I screamed back, and went to check on Salvi, who was zizzing quite happily in the studio. I returned and said to M.A.W., 'Thanks for wanting to kill me and the dogs,' and he said,

'I'll kill you, the dogs and then myself!' A slight improvement.

Meanwhile the ministry types said, 'We have to shoot, we have to obey orders, otherwise there will be a complaint against us and we could get sent to prison, and who would get us out?'

'Do you think dogs will just hang around waiting for you to come and shoot them?' I said. 'You'll never find them, anyway.'

Majeed went with them to the empty lot behind M.A.W.'s house. I told M.A.W. that everyone in the neighbourhood wanted Salvi around to guard the area. 'I don't want any bloody guarding!' he yelled back. Majeed said that the ministry men stayed for around two hours and took a shot at one of the black dogs – Blackie hid until they left. They apparently saw her pups but didn't shoot them, saying, 'Poor things, they too have souls.' They let fly at some birds, which caused a woman with a bad heart who lived right across the road to collapse in a heap. Hamdiya had to go and comfort her. If Salvi is being a menace, then we may have to tie him up more.

The yellow lovebird dropped dead just before they started shooting. Old age perhaps? We went and bought a new blue mate for the white one. We stopped at a shop called 'Birds and Flowers'; they had dogs and a cage with a baby hyena, a Siamese cat and a baby monkey. They seemed to be living happily together, the monkey was jumping on the hyena's back and the cat was curled up fast asleep in a corner. The owner thought the hyena was a pig! Who would want to buy a hyena? They had no birds.

3 June

Apparently, one of the Mauritanian ambassador's ears was cut off by thieves trying to steal his car. Why wasn't there a diplomatic incident? Another diplomat, a Russian woman, was badly cut up in the stomach by another robber, she fought back fiercely and got hit on the head. One of the thieves was caught by neighbours but the others fled. The one who was caught said, 'Why are you bothering? I'll be out in a couple of days.' Meanwhile the Russian lady was taken to hospital and crudely sewn up in the emergency room; later she was operated on properly. She caused a sensation, wandering round the hospital corridors in her underwear – being an attractive lady. There is no air-conditioning working in any of the hospitals and she was hot. She is now recovering inside the Russian embassy.

Surgeons are now operating without gloves. There are none in the country, and the dead have to be buried immediately because there are no working freezers in the hospitals.

Rolf Ekeus came and went without seeing my Destroyer.

We have two broccoli and tomatoes turning orange, what a thrill. Yesterday Majeed proudly showed me a cucumber, at this rate we might feed the nation. The citrus trees seem to have a disease, the oranges drop off when they are the size of ping-pong balls. I have never seen that happen before and it's all over Baghdad, not just in this orchard. Do I have to say goodbye to all my trees?

Majeed has blocked up all of Salvi's exits and has locked him up for the past two days. He is sulking but managed to drag himself into my air-conditioned studio. No sight or sound from M.A.W.'s house, I heard that he wants to leave soon. I'm pleased about that because I was worried about what he would be up to after I leave.

6 June

Isabel said it is the bad environment that is making the oranges fall off the tree; a result of bombs (with barium) dropped during the war. She said that we need to plant four million bombex, ficus and other large leaf trees to improve the quality of the air.

The government can import them from Pakistan, which has a similar climate, at the price of 1 dollar per tree; otherwise all our trees will die. What about us, will we die too, and where are going to get 4 million dollars?

Rushed off to Suha and Assia's house because they had a man there who could put one in a trance under which one answers all questions truthfully. He couldn't put anyone in a trance and was pacing up and down smoking a cigarette. My eyes started to bother me – the cigarette smoke – and I left.

Went to the Saddam Centre to get permission to take Suha and Hisham's portrait out with me to Amman and saw Sulaf there. She too was trying to take out paintings. We didn't have a tape measure and had to approximate the sizes of the canvases – it all has to be officially written down. Also saw Ali Jabiri and we had a great conversation about who was dead/alive and who has left or will leave the country. People seem to be dying like flies. Ali says that if we ask for a permit to die, they'll say, 'Come back in a week and bring all your papers with you.' We would have to pay and then they might refuse our request!

8 June

Everyone had heard about M.A.W.'s scene with the dogs. Sparrows and bees have taken to having baths in the bird bath while magpies and Salvi stand in it and muck about. It's fun watching them all. Yesterday Mahmood said that a dog had gotten into the Ministry of Finance and had to be chased all over the sixth floor. I said maybe he went up in the lift, but Mahmood said it wasn't working. One can imagine the chaos of the scene. Iraqis are scared of dogs.

Another sad story. A lady I met at Amal's last week has been killed, her husband shot and their car stolen from near the old British Council. Amal is in a sad state and unable to work on embroidering her son's wedding bed-cover – another delay for a wedding that never seems to take place.

Went to see Hajir, buried in the past of her albums and photos. She gave away her magazines from 1910 to Abla Jalila, who is one of the few people left in Baghdad who can read old Turkish. Pictures of our noble ancestors. Hajir doesn't enjoy looking at the past so much now, she's getting very thin and doesn't have the energy to do anything, not even let in the man coming to mend her air-conditioner. She rarely comes downstairs but stays up in her limbo on the first floor.

Isabel thinks that men's sperm count is less and weaker and that is why there is such a high mortality rate of babies. It's not only malnutrition, but also the after-effects of the mineral fallout – the uranium, barite, etc – from the Gulf War.

11 June

Gave a big dinner last night and again did not manage to have a proper conversation with anyone. Mila and Kawthar liked their portrait very much, a big relief. I'm always very nervous with sitters before they see the end result. I made a huge amount of Bloody Marys, using fresh tomatoes, but I put in too much chilli powder – people were choking on it – and there were not many takers. A huge quantity was left over. I bottled it and put it in the fridge. Amal came in very fancy, high-heeled shoes that looked like perspex pyramids. Halfway through dinner one of the heels came apart, so I told her that I would stick it for her and gave her a pair of slippers to go home in. She was wearing an embroidered Palestinian dress and said, 'Don't you remember this dress? It was eaten by rats when I was staying at your house during the war.' Amal gave it to some Palestinian lady to repair and she cut out the eaten pieces and repatched it. It has no back now (presumably that went to patch up the front), so she wears it with a jacket.

Dhafir has a story that he has told us many times, but which seems to be more factual every day. The time is February 1993, when Dhafir was in Somalia working as a doctor for the UN forces (I was in London waiting for *Granta* to come out). Mutaza, in Baghdad, was driving the car taking Ma and Needles to a *futtur* dinner at Sahira's house (it was Ramadhan). As they were driving, a horrific storm blew up that turned everything orange and black. By the time they left to go back home, the car was covered with black dust and mud that they had to wipe off to be able to see. It was also difficult to breathe. A couple of weeks later, Dhafir was sitting with his fellow workers in the dark in Somalia (no electricity) and each was telling a story. An American with them told them about how he had been exploding warheads that day and that this time they had done it properly. Apparently they have to dig a huge, deep hole, line the interior with a steel and concrete frame, put in the stuff that has to be exploded, and then seal it with cement so that the dust of the explosion stays buried for generations. In Iraq, he continued to tell them, we had a similar assignment – to blow up war materials. When he went to the site, he noticed that there was no concrete bunker or even a built structure, just a hole in the ground. When he radioed to his superiors and informed them of this, they told him not to bother with safety measures and just to explode the material regardless. Everyone knew there was a big storm coming from the south but they blew up the warheads anyway. He wrote up a report and sent it to headquarters, so presumably it is part of the sea of unread files in the UN. He then went on to tell them that in the coming two to four years, there will be a terrible increase in cancer, leukaemia, glaucoma, bone and joint problems in Iraq. Trees and plants will suffer too, although a few may flourish. Fruit will fall off the trees and it will be an environmental disaster. Dhafir couldn't remember the man's name, but says he has it somewhere among his papers and will look it up.

The UN will keep the embargo until all Iraqis are dead. They are always finding new stories and blaming us. Now all this stuff in the warehouse in New York – nuclear material stolen from the Ukraine, imported into the USA under the eyes of US

Customs and then bought by Iraqi agents so that the country can continue to work on its nuclear bomb. How far-fetched can a story get? All this, with the UN commission visiting every two months to check on our military capabilities – we're supposed to be building a bomb under their very noses. Either we are geniuses or else the UN commissions are made up of a bunch of imbeciles. The whole thing is such a charade.

Back to M.A.W., who has been on another rampage. He told Hashim, 'Please talk to that dog and keep her busy while I go and get my gun' – the dog he was referring to was Salvi's black wife, mum of a million pups. Naturally she had disappeared by the time he got back, so Majeed went with him while he fired a couple of rounds. M.A.W. is now building a high wall along one side of his house, but the road end is so low the dogs will be able to jump over it easily. Serves him right. I'm not talking to him.

14 June

The UN man in Somalia was a senior field officer in the UN Department for Humanitarian Affairs. Dhafir looked him up. How do you like that? The humanitarian bit is what gets me every time. He didn't know that Dhafir was only out of Iraq for a short while and would return, and when he found out he said, 'Gosh, I shouldn't have told you that; now you will tell everyone,' and Dhafir said he would not tell. I have told this story to Isabel and she will include it in her report. She told me that she had been asked to go and check the area around Eridu, a most beautiful archaeological site near the Saudi border. The ground is covered with some sort of silver glaze, and there is no one to check it – Isabel thinks it might be mercury. There are mines in the area but the government doesn't have the money or the experts to get rid of them.

Kristoff's Mercedes has been stolen. The driver left the car to buy a paper, leaving the key in the ignition. One second later the car was gone. Now he's in prison because they have to check whether he was part of a gang of thieves. Each embassy is allowed to have three cars and they had just bought a new one and were going to sell this one. The same thing happened five years ago – the car was stolen just before it was due to be sold. It was the same driver, too. Smells fishy. Isabel says a lot of the embassies are being harassed; the French have had rocks thrown at them and at their windows. I can't blame people too much if there is resentment.

We took the Destroyer to Samira's farm. It looked very happy sitting in the open countryside. She said she would paint it whenever it needed it, and I said I would keep adding to it. When I told Suha, she said, 'You know where you've taken it? – right next to the nuclear power plant that was bombed by the Israelis years ago.' Isn't that funny? Without premeditation, it has gone to defend – although it's against my principles to have anything atomic around. Anyway, the Destroyer can't function as anything much.

Mudhaffar talked to us about the chaos in the city's hospitals – no air-conditioning, overpowering heat, patients running away because they can't bear it, but returning sicker than when they left – a nightmare that has to be seen to be believed. A lot of massive heart attacks among the young, twenty years old or so, and a virus that they think may be encephalitis because of its symptoms – it kills in two days – but there is no pathology lab to do post-mortems.

M.A.W. put out poison for the dogs, so I had to tie up Salvi tonight. Majeed says he saw him in the afternoon fighting a big black snake.

15 June

There are three dead dogs according to Majeed, including two mums, ex-Salvi wives, poor pups. Hamdiya saved a whole pile of pups by keeping them around her house. She tells them not to go to M.A.W.'s house and somehow they obey her. They remain very quietly inside the fenced area of the orchard.

I need to have my bones checked; all my joints hurt. Dhafir said that it's part of Gulf War Syndrome. The BBC said that there was some sort of military coup, but it all seems very quiet and no one knows anything. Few armed guards around. The government has naturally denied all.

16 June

I was supposed to be leaving today, but am still here and it looks like I will not be able to leave for at least another week. I am determined not to pay the 200,000-dinar exit fee tax, and as an artist going to have an exhibition, I am supposed to be exempted from paying it. But I can't wait too long. I have only two and a half months in Amman to do the objects for my exhibition there.

Went to see Hassan about my aching bones. He took five X-rays plus blood tests – the results come out tomorrow. I told him I just wanted to know whether it was old age or something that one could do something about.

We had the first anniversary of Waloodie's death, a cancer victim. I was not in Baghdad when he died but he didn't want to die as he had so much to do still. 'Why me?' he kept saying. How we all miss him, a lovely man.

My wrists are hurting from too much typing. I am falling apart at the seams. Apparently something did happen yesterday but it's all very hush-hush.

Exams are nearly over and all those who paid bribes have passed. They didn't have to study. There is a set fee that one pays to the teacher and, regardless of the grade, one passes. That even goes for the baccalaureate. A quarter of a million dinars for the exam questions – who cares about learning?

Neighbours are complaining about the smell of dead dogs. I said it has nothing to do with me. It's all M.A.W.'s fault, he was the one who reported on the dogs and he should be responsible for burying them. The shopkeepers on the corner are giving milk to the dogs so they won't die from the poison, and now Majeed says black wife didn't die; maybe she was just ill. Everyone avoids M.A.W. now, even his friends don't seem to be coming round any more.

It's a relief to know that I'm not the only artist waiting for an exit permit. Ismail says all the big artists are waiting. I'm honoured to be considered a big artist. Maybe they think there will be a big exodus of artists out of the country and that we won't come back, like the university professors who had to sell their very lives to leave, poor buggers. We artists have always been given a free rein, otherwise we wouldn't have lasted all this while.

17 June

The word 'big' in Arabic also has the connotation of 'old' (in age). I think that's more like it; the young offer challenge and energy.

I'm trying to get away with paying 25,000 dinars. I made 200,000 dinars in my exhibition so it's peanuts to pay out for leaving. I still see no reason to give it all to the government.

My problems are with my back. My old scoliosis has returned and I can't blame it on the Americans.

I wish there was some way to lay a complaint, a plea or even a cry for help in the name of all those who have died from wars or become sick in the aftermath – to move the conscience of the world to make it a better place to live in. Why can't the USA stop selling arms and make money out of better things? Can one plant arms, eat or sleep with them? I wish someone could give me a rational answer.

Had an exciting false alarm when they rang and said that my exit papers were in order and to come to the ministry. But alas, they were only beginning the process, not finishing it, and I had to fill out a whole lot of forms about whether I was a Ba'thi or not, etc. If they hurry the procedure, it may be finished in a week to ten days.

While I was making photocopies in a shop, I looked out of the window and saw a few sparrows. One of them had no tail, but all of a sudden it took off and flew away. So I said to the owner of the shop that the bird had no tail, so how could it fly? He answered, 'Don't worry, the whole population of Iraq is in that same position and they are surviving.' The bird will survive, too; it will not have a good guidance sense, it will have difficulty with balancing, in turning right or left, but it will survive. I thought it was the most appropriate and descriptive metaphor of the present state of the people of Iraq.

Baghdad, June 1995

Exile

23 June 1995 – Amman

I now have a thumb print on my passport instead of a signature. I came out as an illiterate – that way, one can leave without paying an extra million. They took 150 dollars from me at the border. I was given a receipt for it, supposedly one gets refunded when one returns. Every time one leaves Iraq, it involves melodrama and endless humiliation. One wonders why one ever returns. Memory playing tricks again.

The first thing all Iraqis do upon arrival in Amman is to make a beeline for various doctors' waiting rooms – each to their own particular ailments. Once that has been taken care of, they queue up for visas. Any embassy will do.

4 July

I have been undergoing millions of tests for my bone-marrow problems – my blood tests show I have low platelets, somewhere in the 80s. Nobody will tell me what I have. Is it cancer? Tomorrow I have to have more tests. Went to work in very low spirits. I have been given space at the gallery, Darat al-Funun, where I can do the work for my coming exhibition. Lovely outdoor spaces and terraces where I can put all my stones and metal bits. This complex of old houses used to belong to the British authorities and T.E. Lawrence often came to tea here.

Picked up an interesting rock in the garden and under it was this huge scorpion with a big green belly and black pincers and tail. They are the only things I'm terrified of and so thought it must be a bad omen. Azar came and touched it with his foot. It moved, and he squashed it. 'It's gone now,' he said, but I couldn't work any more so came home to write and get it out of my system.

My doctor said that I have a murmur in my throat and a thickening of the arteries. 'Do you smoke?' he asked.

'It's from the bloody pollution and other people's cigarettes,' I said. I hope that I pop off quickly and don't linger around in an ill way. I wish I could blame it all on the USA; the scoliosis may be pushing it, but there should be no problem with the pollution.

12 August
The BBC is comparing Saddam to King Lear and his daughters. I like that. The situation in Amman is electric; one can actually feel it. Iraqis no longer talk about their illnesses, only about what is going to happen. I didn't believe it when I was first told about the daughters skipping out of Iraq with husbands and kids, etc.* I thought it was yet another rumour, but I turned out to be wrong, yet again. The order of priority for conversations among Iraqis abroad now is: first, the latest rumours about Hussein Kamel and the daughters; then their own diseases; third is immigration; and fourth is the search to find a job anywhere, but especially in Jordan, Yemen or Libya, the only countries that don't require entry visas for Iraqis.

Every other person working at the Darat is an Iraqi on the way out, waiting for the clearance of papers to Sweden, Australia, Canada, New Zealand, Malaysia or even Holland. It's tragic. They are all young and want to make a new life for

---

*   Saddam Hussein's two daughters, together with their husbands and children, fled to Jordan in August 1995.

themselves elsewhere. I sit here like an old crone, giving advice, filling out forms for them and writing petitions. I can't tell them not to go – everyone needs a chance in this life and what chance have they in Iraq? It will be centuries before that country is normal again.

22 August

The impact of my exhibition was fantastic, but I'm not sure about sales. There is a poet here at the Darat, and yesterday he asked me, 'You mean these stones and tin cans of yours are for sale?'

I was very miffed and said, 'Well, for a poet you certainly don't seem to have much imagination.'

More and more Iraqis are coming out, including a weedy-looking artist who said that he had come out for medical treatment. 'So what's new?' I said. I have not written about my medical problems. Q kicked up a terrific fuss when he heard about my low platelets and I had to have hundreds of extra blood tests and a horrid bone-marrow test. No one can find anything except a nasty throat infection. My platelets are still low. Freako thinks it's the tension – that can cause a low platelet count too.

30 August

Phoned the Pakistani embassy to find out whether I needed a visa to go there. 'We can't issue it from here,' he said. 'You either get it in Baghdad or we have to write and get permission from Pakistan.' Even Pakistan is playing hard to get. I suppose I'll have to pull strings.

Journalists are paying a lot of attention to me. They read about an exhibition by an Iraqi artist, called 'Embargo Art', and came in droves. Usually they don't like what I say. It doesn't suit their purpose. The CNN correspondent was totally uninterested in my art. She just wanted to know whether all Iraqis were rallying around Hussein Kamel. 'What for?' I said. 'But I will explain some of my sculptures to you if you don't censor what I say. These particular sculptures are made of large coiled springs from lorries that I have painted to look like snakes; inside these coiled springs are a few stones painted to look like animals. The snakes symbolize dictatorship.' I told her they swallow people whole, not just our sort of dictatorship but all of them, yours included. 'In fact,' I added, 'yours is the biggest of all because it has swallowed up the whole world.'

7 September

The situation seems to have calmed down a bit and everyone has gotten used to the way things are. Hussein Kamel has been forgotten, hidden away somewhere in the palace grounds, the talk is back to medical problems and diseases. At lunch yesterday at Nazha's I heard some lovely stories from her cousins who have been living in exile in London for many years. They talked of Baghdad in the old days and of the first midwife, *circa* early 1930s, who went round in a carriage wearing a large hat. Her Mercedes was also her ambulance, Nazha said, and as kids they used to follow her round.

Heard about a nasty incident that befell Abla Jalila in her house in Baghdad – some men came in pretending to be security types and started to look around. She said that she didn't have much and offered them cigarettes. They put a gun to her head and told her to hand over everything. She showed them where she had hidden 5,000 dinars (which is nothing much) and they went all over the house looking for anything worthwhile to take. Found all the maid's gold jewellery, took that and left. Abla Jalila had to pay her maid the cost price of the gold. She was lucky they didn't kill her.

20 September

Spent the morning sitting in the Intercontinental Hotel with Khaldun and listening to his stories. A friend of his went to a butcher to buy some meat and saw a man behind the counter cutting meat very slowly. 'Who is this?' he asked the owner.

'Oh,' he answered, 'just an Iraqi surgeon without a job, trying his luck at this one.' Another Iraqi, an aeronautical engineer, serves coffee in an art gallery. We went on to discuss our favourite topic – health, or rather lack of it, as one grows older and bits of one's body stop functioning properly. Khaldun said that Virginia Woolf started a diary describing each deficiency as it started, but she didn't live long enough. He told us that his mother only got herself eyeglasses after she hung her coat on what she thought was a coat-hanger, but which turned out to be a fly on the wall. It flew in her face.

Faiza has broken her leg in three places and is in a plaster cast – she has to stay in it for six weeks.

17 November – Beirut

I'm not certain what Ma is wearing. She's turning her old shirts and dresses into cushions, but her skirt actually looks like a cushion. So I asked her whether she was wearing one and she said, 'It's good silk, isn't it?'

Ma came across an Iraqi who works in a bakery and he gave her a letter to take to his family in Baghdad when she goes back. When he tried to call them from Beirut they refused to take the call or even acknowledge his existence. Apparently, he'd already been declared a war hero and his family has taken (and spent?) the cash bonus for a war martyr – they didn't want to know him any more. He wants Ma to talk to his sister because she may be more sympathetic to his plight. Poor man, he ran away from the army and has been cut off from family and friends for six years – he cannot even be put on an immigration or amnesty list. It's too late.

12 December

Dood just phoned and said that I sounded pretty cheerful. I don't know why because I am hounded by leaking and/or blocked water pipes. Have been trying to repair our bathroom, which got a rocket hit during the civil war. We now have a shiny new Italian bathtub – at least we don't have to shower in that rusty bin as we were doing before. But the drip from the bathroom continues. I set up an elaborate contraption to trap this drip but it will not oblige, and continues to go straight down the wall. The floor is always wet. It's been pouring with rain and the balconies are flooded with five inches of water. The men who came to put in the bathtub mixed the cement on the balcony and blocked up the drains. Stupid idiots. I've already had to wade out twice to try to unblock them. I managed to get the water down by about three inches.

I went to the bakery to tell the runaway Iraqi that I couldn't get through to Baghdad to speak to Ma; the lines are down. Found another Iraqi there – his father died because there were no medicines. He left Baghdad with only one year to go before graduating with a BA. He wanted to commit suicide, but said it's a sin. 'I sometimes don't have enough to eat, I'm 30 years old and what is there in life for me?' I told him we all had to leave and earn money in the outside world in whatever way we could. They won't let me pay for the bread in this bread shop full of Iraqis.

20 December
Mini told us the following story, and I can't resist repeating it. During the civil war in Beirut, a Tarzan film was showing to a packed movie house when in walks a fundamentalist-looking type with a loaded gun and sits down. When Tarzan put his hand on Jane's thigh, this guy stood up and yelled, 'Take your hands off the girl!' Of course, Tarzan paid no attention, so the fundamentalist took up his gun, aimed and started shooting at Tarzan. Everyone in the cinema was terrified and crouched down under their seats. The film died, and slowly the place

emptied. I said, 'That's a beautiful story, but it must be apocryphal.'

'No,' she said, 'my cousin was in the audience.'

Beirut is much safer these days. There has been much improvement since I was here last year. It may even be the safest place to live in the Middle East. Instead of guns, everyone carries mobile phones – *le cellulaire* as they are called here. They ring in cinemas, at funerals, in handbags ... The streets echo to the sound of 'allo, allo'. They don't function well inside buildings. A Lebanese simply cannot be seen in a car without one clutched in their hand, even though there's a fine for driving and talking at the same time, but who cares here?

Went to Christmas mass with Magda and her Buddhist maid – an English mass for Filipinos. Guitars were playing, Sri Lankans singing and dancing a most pagan-looking dance, all in front of a statue of Christ. The priest looked stunned and amazed. The Filipino congregation sang and we all held hands and sang for peace in this world.

15 January 1996

Can't wait for the summer to come because there's a new waterproof *cellulaire* telephone, and I can just see the Lebanese drowning by the hundreds as they try to press buttons/numbers and swim with no hands.

Phoned Ma and Needles in Baghdad. They sounded utterly distraught. I felt guilty being here. When I'm in Baghdad I shunt them around in the car and make them laugh. There is no cheer left there, what with Tawadud dead and Dhafir in a bad way.

Iraqis are not good at immigrating. Being virtually landlocked, immigration to them is a serious matter, one that's been almost forced on them for the last twenty-five years. On the other hand, generations of Lebanese have gotten into boats and sailed across the world and settled from the Americas to Africa, quite happily.

There are nearly 150 different Iraqi opposition groups (*muaradha*) in exile, typical of such an individualistic people. How the hell can anything get done, and when they do get together they just quarrel and sling accusations at each other. Childish remarks such as, 'Your hands are steeped in blood' or 'You were seen cocktailing at the Iraqi embassy the other day.' Bitchy and stupid for the most part. They squabble about every detail: whether one can have a revolution without a policy or strategy, or whether it's simply better to get rid of the ruler and hope for the best. History has consistently shown us that when Iraqis knock off their leaders, what follows is usually much worse. Then they can feel even sorrier for themselves.

22 January
Asked friends and fellow exiles at lunch today what they thought about that state. Atta spent thirteen years in prison, five of them under sentence of death, so I asked him how exile compares with being inside. He thought a minute and said, 'You're free there at least ... But I consider myself no better off than a garbage collector or sweeper here. Since I can read and write, I have a job that allows me to survive – I take what comes my way ... In the end, I took the decision to leave because I knew that I wouldn't be able to survive financially in Baghdad. We would have had to start selling off our things and in the end we'd have been left with nothing to sell. At least now we're surviving.'

His wife is another matter. She said, 'I don't have work, my things are not around me, we live in a rented flat. I'm bored and at a loose end. The family is dispersed and what am I supposed to do with myself?'

Balchis said she was happy anywhere. Rifat said, 'Iraq is the source of my inspiration. Yes, I would go back. I would live nine months of the year there and the rest abroad. Because I write, I can rely on myself. It has been OK.' When Rifat was in prison in Baghdad, a security guard asked him to come with him for questioning. Rifat told him to come back for him after 11 o'clock (he never talks before that time – just works). The guard did not persist. Rifat is rather imperious and can get away with such behaviour. When they finally let him out of prison his response was, 'Too bad. I needed another three months to finish my book.'

Phoned up Needles. She seemed OK but depressed. (Ma was not there. Abu Ali came and took her to my house to get rid of a rat.) I asked Needles how Qusay was faring, and she said that by the time he got a visa to go to the USA, he had only three days to live. He died in hospital, too late. Assia left Baghdad and now has a job in Libya teaching English for 250 dollars a month. How can she manage? She has finally given up cigarettes and gotten fat – probably couldn't afford them on her salary. Exile does have some side benefits.

6 February – Amman
Sitting in the Iraqi embassy this morning, waiting for them to renew my passport (there's no Iraqi embassy in Lebanon, so we have to go to Jordan for all official transactions), I started chatting to a man, a poet who is taking his PhD in literature. He had spent six months earning his living as a taxi-driver in Baghdad. 'Did you write any taxi poems?' I asked.

'Twelve,' he replied, 'but most of them can't be published now. Only one will be.' He said artists and creative people have to escape repressive regimes because they need to produce. That's certainly true for Iraqi artists. They are all out now.

The Iraqi *dinar* went from 2,500 to 200 to the US dollar at the mere hint of the embargo being lifted! All in the space of a few days. Some people lost millions. I doubt that the embargo will be lifted.

I have started to ask Iraqi friends in Jordan what they feel about exile. Uns said, 'I don't even think of it.'

Her husband Salwan said simply, 'I'm lost.'

7 February

Got my passport renewed. It was fairly easy, but I got badly mauled at the Lebanese embassy. The guard first asked me where my husband was and I told him that was none of his business. Then he cursed all Iraqis and said, 'Saturday is the day for Iraqis,' and slammed the door in my face. Why do we have to take this shit?

I walked to the Intercontinental Hotel for a bit of cheer to see Khaldun, who holds court there every morning. 'Exile!' he said. 'I've always been in exile. First as a kid with King Faisal when the French came in and we had to leave Syria, then from Iraq. I don't know any other way of life. But I'll tell you the story of a desk. My maternal grandfather got a desk from his mother from America. When they moved to Syria they took the desk with them. When they were expelled from there in 1920 the desk remained behind and disappeared.

'Years later,' he continued, 'my father passed through Damascus and saw the desk in a friend's house. They had bought it in an antique shop and insisted that he take the desk. So he took it to Baghdad.' Where is that desk now? Perhaps with Selwa.

8 February

Hazzema said that outside one's homeland one is a nobody. The need to remember specific scenes, smells and the atmospheres of the past is always with one, but these particulars don't exist any more. One has exiled oneself from them – but one still keeps looking back.

Mubajal said, 'Ever since I was a child, all my life, I've been in exile. Now finally I have decided to exile myself in exile.' It's true, she never leaves her house. Even the doctor has to pay house calls.

Freako said she will continue to fight and argue against what has happened to all of us. 'I saw it coming twenty years ago,'

she said, 'and I took the decision to leave. But I'm still angry.'
Red Cross statistics say that three and a half million Iraqis have
emigrated in the last ten years – two million in the last five
years.

13 February

Sina misses his house terribly. 'I lived in the same house all my
life,' he said. 'I know every corner of it. Here we have to pay
rent. I'm not used to that. I'd go back like a shot if there was the
slightest hope for a future.' His brother Lahab does not agree
because he thinks being in Jordan is not really exile as we're so
close to the Jordanians. I completely disagree with that
statement – not the people, not the country, not the trees, not
the buildings, not the stones, not the customs and habits, not
even the Arabic is the same – it's a different dialect. And
definitely not the climate or the people. They are placid and we
are most volatile – the same goes for the climate.

My Lebanese visa was refused so I had to pull strings.
Françoise and Cecil managed to get me an interview with the
ambassador. One would think that after suffering for twenty
years as a pariah nation, the Lebanese would be slightly more
sympathetic towards others going through the same process.
One certainly gets one's fill of humiliation. The nasty guard was
again rude to me. When I told him that I had an appointment
with the ambassador, he yelled out my name loudly on the
intercom and then added as an aside, 'The artist'. Instantly,
heads turned to look at me and they all smirked. The guard was
very disappointed when they informed him that I did have an
appointment. The ambassador gave me a hard time too. In fact,
I thought he was going to refuse to give me a re-entry permit,
but finally he said that for the sake of Françoise he would. We
talked a bit about art and then he finally gave it to me. Hurrah.

Himmat is working on an exhibition at the Darat and has
been shuffling between Paris and Tokyo for the last few years.
He said that one is oneself whatever the place. He misses

specific things but has only a few belongings that he leaves with a friend when he's travelling. When he finishes this exhibition, he will return to Paris. 'How will you get a visa?' I asked.

'Oh, that's the easy part,' he answered. I forgot that he's a Kurd and for them visas are not a problem. Kurds and Christian Iraqis get preferential treatment, ordinary Iraqi Muslims are the West's public enemy number one. Kurds are only refused visas to Arab countries – isn't that extraordinary? He said that Paris is full of Iraqi artists who should have stayed at home. At least they were respected there. In Paris they do manual work, meet in cafés and talk of home. Time has stood still for them, lost in and between both worlds. They miss the life of extended families, now scattered across continents.

15 February

May says it's all a question of identity. One doesn't have to go around proving oneself all the time when one's at home. She doesn't feel so homesick in Amman because she lives in a building full of Iraqis. She hears their music, and their talk is all round her. She works as an independent scholar doing her own research, so it may be easier for her than for her husband Rafi, who teaches at the university. It's a bureaucratic job and he isn't happy. However, his life cannot be compared to those who emigrated to New Zealand in search of a new passport and work. They are truly cut off from their roots, their link to the past tenuous at best. How long would it take to save for a return ticket home?

There is hardly an Iraqi who has come to Jordan and who has relaxed – here to stay. Getting a work or residence permit is nearly impossible. It's not really Jordan's fault. They are a small country and have overstretched their capacity. Even if one gets a job here it's for low pay and there aren't many prospects. Insecurity and vulnerability are permanent conditions; most Iraqis would return if things were right again in Iraq.

May told me the story of one of her Basra relatives who came to stay with them in Baghdad after the war. One of her daughters had a bad attack of asthma and died because they couldn't get her oxygen fast enough. Her mother's reaction in grief was, 'Why did she have to die in foreign lands?' Baghdad is only a few hundred kilometres north of Basra yet she felt that she was not at home. Exile is a state of mind.

Got a letter from Ma. Apparently, the day that she went to check my house for a lurking rat, she forgot to turn off one of the lights upstairs. The next morning Majeed showed up early on her doorstep and told her that Salvi had been driving him crazy. All night long he chased round and round the house, going to the garage, then to the front door and back again, in a complete frenzy. He must have thought I was back home, or that something was going on in the house, and he was trying to warn Majeed. Ma said she almost cried for poor Salvi.* I felt sad all day.

It seems that Hussein Kamel and his brother each have a son called Saddam. They are both at school in Amman.

More stories from Baghdad. Chaos ensued when the *dinar* suddenly soared in value. People went on crazy buying sprees as food prices plummeted. The banks remained open all night long so that people could exchange their hoarded dollars for the dreaded dinars that they had not been keeping. I smell a rat – the government was the clear winner. People rushed to the market and bought sheep, thousands of them; so many slaughtered, a grizzly sight. There may not be enough lambs born next spring. On top of that, not enough farmers planted grain this year because the *dinar* had plummeted at seed-buying time and the government didn't lower the prices. Most farmers could not afford to buy expensive seed, so they left their fields fallow. Yaki lost a lot of money on his potato crop. He

---

*   Salvi was left in Baghdad to look after the orchard in the author's absence.

borrowed from the bank to install his cold-storage plants. When the time came to sell the potatoes, his price was too high. He had to sell for the normal price and lost a lot more.

Apparently there is little cash left in the banks; they give out pieces of paper, like IOUs. People who bring their grain to government depots are getting free fridges and washing machines instead of cash!

Ramadhan in Amman is a desolate business. People work for two hours a day and whenever one asks for anything, they say, 'Come back when Ramadhan is over.' The whole month is shot. In Beirut prices shot up astronomically during Ramadhan and when one asked why, they answered, 'Because it's Ramadhan and people can eat that much more.'

16 February

Went to Ghor al-Himma, to Mamduh's beautiful hot springs oasis. It borders the Golan. Before Syria was their neighbour, now it's Israel. Freako and Rabab went for a walk to the border while I was swimming, and chatted up the guards. The fence is wired on the Israeli side, but the Jordanians can't afford to electrify their fences so they man them with soldiers. No peace agreement seems to have been signed for this border, nothing has changed here. Mamduh told us a lovely story. One morning, one of his workers brought him a couple of lychees he said he had picked up from under the fig tree. When he told him that that was not possible, the workman insisted that that's where he'd picked them up. So Mamduh went to check. Sure enough, bits and pieces of half-eaten lychees littered the ground under the Ficus. He looked around and saw that there was a row of lychee trees planted on the Israeli side. Further investigation uncovered a colony of bats who cross the border nightly, pick the lychees and bring them back to Jordan to eat. I wondered whether the bats were pro-Jordanian and/or whether they would continue to behave in a similar manner once the Golan was returned to the Syrians. I also wondered whether they would stop crossing the border once Mamduh's lychee trees begin to bear fruit. It would be interesting to follow up this story. The bats may simply be enjoying their freedom to move, their liberty as against the lack of it for humans.

During and after lunch, the talk was endlessly about work and residence permits, visas and identities. Mamduh said that maybe the easiest way for us to travel now would be by hijacking aeroplanes! We were a mixed bunch of Lebanese, Jordanians, Palestinians and Iraqis, every one of us chasing bits of paper – so much effort for a licence to live.

19 February

Back in Beirut after the usual messy scrum of airports and travelling. Why can't passports and borders be abolished? Crooks seem to manage, regardless of restrictions; ordinary people who don't know how to get round are the true sufferers. Just talked to Ma, who is still stuck in Baghdad. The government has not yet changed the cost of an exit permit, 400,000 dinars. At the old rate it means over 900 dollars to get out. Who can afford that? She won't come 'til May. Maybe by then they will have adjusted the price, otherwise she'll have to borrow the money. She sounded depressed and has a fever. Needles sounded worse. Dhafir has left the hospital and gone home because the government closed it down – something to do with illegal workers. Imagine shutting down a whole hospital and sending everyone home. Everything there sounds dismal.

I went to check on the Iraqis at the bakery. The one who gave his home phone number in Baghdad to Ma has disappeared. He went into a complete frenzy, fearing that we were going to rat on him (to whom, I wonder?), and up and left the shop. He hasn't been seen since. Poor guy.

Went and saw Atta and Batool. He is just out of hospital and seems well. He told me a lovely story that was published in the *Hayat* newspaper today. Apparently, an Iraqi had agreed with his parents on a special code that he would use when he made good his escape from Iraq. The code went as follows: once he was out, he would phone and say that he had arrived in Iran. This meant that he was safely out. If he said that he had moved to a new house, it meant that he'd managed to get to Sweden as an immigrant. They also decided that he should have a new name – Zuhair (his real name was Qais). So when he got to Sweden, he phoned his mother and said, 'Hello Ma, this is Zuhair speaking.'

'What Zuhair?' she said.

'Just Zuhair,' he answered.

'Oh,' she replied, 'you think I can't recognize your voice. You're Qais. Where are you?' So he said,

'I've gone away.' 'I know,' she said, 'you left Iran.'

He thought quickly and decided that if he said he'd moved to a new house, she might remember that this conversation was supposed to be in code, so he said, 'I've moved to a new home.'

'I know,' she said. 'You've gone to Sweden.' By then the father had realized what was happening and grabbed the telephone from his wife's hand, and she suddenly remembered that it was supposed to be their code. She had forgotten ...

The latest story of hardships from Baghdad: the soaring prices of foodstuffs and the shortages have now hit the zoo. Bananas were never cheap in Baghdad, even at the best of times, but now their price is so prohibitive that the zoo can't afford them. So monkeys are being fed with carrots instead. They don't like carrots and fling them, one by one, at passers-by. Lions won't eat carrots, so old donkeys are being killed and their meat given to the lions.

All conversations rotate round the subject of Hussein Kamel and his brother. Is it really possible that they have asked to go back? He started out in life as a driver and then rose through the ranks to become the third most important person in the country. Then he left and became a non-entity, a nothing, maybe even a liability. Gossip has it that King Hussein wants his palace back and/or that Hussein Kamel is missing his own palace in Baghdad. In the meantime, political affiliations have changed so much in Amman that even the *muaradha*, the opposition, is setting up shop here.

21 February

I can't believe it – that stupid Hussein Kamel has gone back to Baghdad.* I've come to the conclusion that Iraqis must be the most unpredictable people in the world.

24 February

Sol arrived, but not her baggage. It's either stuck in Amman or in Yemen.

I knew that the brothers would be knocked off, but I didn't think it would be so immediate. I thought Saddam would belittle them a bit, maybe even give back Hussein Kamel his old job as a driver. Saddam said that he was going to treat them like ordinary Iraqis. Well, wasn't that an appropriate description of what happened to them! It's obvious what Hussein Kamel thought about exile – he couldn't take it. But to the extent that he was willing to chance going back to his father-in-law?

25 February

I was doing my back exercise this morning, lying on the floor and looking up at a spider on the ceiling. He seemed as nervous as I was, and when I got to the bicycling exercise he went hysterical, rushing round in all directions. Imagine what his eyes saw – legs rolling round and round, coming closer to him and retreating. By the time I'd finished, I was relieved to see that he was cowering in a corner. Long, fine legs – I hate spiders. They

---

*   In February 1996 Hussein Kamel al-Majid and his brother, Saddam Kamel al-Majid (both sons-in-law of Saddam Hussein), returned with their families to Iraq after a brief exile in Jordan. They were both divorced by their wives and were killed soon afterwards.

remind me of the convent days in Simla; our loos there were permanently occupied by large, hairy spiders that lay hidden and surprised one when one began to relax.

Atta also heard the rumour that Saddam's sons-in-law had left their kids behind in Amman. They could have been considered sons of traitors.

We called Ma. She said that they had a very tiring day yesterday. Must have been tense with all these goings-on. They were told nothing but the official version, not that we know that much more on the outside. I wonder where Hussein Kamel's father's house is in Baghdad.

1 March

Well it's done. Forty-five people killed after a five-hour siege; grandchildren too, if the reports are correct. The house flattened. What happens to the daughters now? They can't appreciate having their husbands killed, divorcing them was another matter. I wonder what really happened.

2 March

Drama last night at 11.30. I went into my bedroom, switched on the light and saw a giant tarantula on the wall, black and furry. I screamed and Sol came running from her bed. We fetched brooms and hovered around. It was pouring with rain outside and the spider might have come in for shelter. Sol asked why the cats didn't eat it. I said, 'They have better taste.' There are more than seven resident cats on our balconies. I feed them. My favourite is happily asleep in his cardboard box. He sleeps while I paint, and we chat on occasion. The birds get fed separately on Sol's balcony, so that the cats won't eat them. Sol says it's like living in a menagerie.

Anyway, the tarantula was not welcome. Sol was braver than me. I asked her whether she had her glasses on because I didn't want it to fall on me. Suddenly I heard footsteps coming down the stairs. I ran and opened our front door and saw a youth descending. I asked him whether he felt brave. 'Yes,' he said, so I asked him to help us. We handed him a couple of brooms and he carried out his task efficiently. He took the tarantula away between two planks of wood. We thanked him profusely. We don't know who he was. Of course, I couldn't sleep a wink after that. I watched two films on TV.

This morning two furry, broken legs were all that remained on the floor – a terrible reminder – as if one could forget.

4 March

Sol said I have to end with a proper finale. I can't end this diary on a spider note.

So what is exile? My father died in exile in Beirut in 1971 and Ma thought to take him back and bury him in Baghdad, which she did. Does it make a difference? I myself want to be buried wherever I die. I dislike the West temporarily for making us suffer more than we already have, and so will keep myself and my travels limited to the East. Not that the West is dying for my company. It's a kind of self-imposed or -inflicted embargo, a little gesture. Sol brought Mahasti to dinner last night. She said she found exile hard to take. There is a purpose and a pride that you lose when you don't have a country. That purpose means you are acknowledged, recognized. In the outside world you're nothing, you have to constantly introduce and reintroduce yourself. You start from scratch every time: 'Who are you? Where are you from? What do you do?'

'Look at me,' she continued. 'I love my job and I'd never have been able to do such work at home, but we are rootless, floating and all alone.' She took one look at my work and said that my artwork is 'world art'.

'What's that?' I asked.

'No barriers,' she said. 'You talk right across.' She's quite right. I feel no barriers. I can work anywhere, live anywhere and be influenced by anywhere. When I returned from Pakistan, I couldn't stop myself from putting sequins and glittery studs on everything, but after two months, here I am, gradually becoming more Lebanonized, if there is such a word.

Mahasti says the future lies with the New-Age children – the environmentally conscious generation. 'Do you think they will not be corrupted too?' I asked. 'People get corrupted once in power.'

'Well, at least a few good things will filter through them, it's as much as one can hope for,' she replied.

Communication is so easy now. Look at the Internet. A couple have even been married over the Internet. Even the bats in Mamduh's orchard worked it out to their advantage, science and nature. It's bloody politicians who need to have borders to protect their territories. They need to be reborn. When will we be civilized enough to be able to trust each other? Look at our immediate family: Sol is off to New York in a few days, Kiko is in Urbana, Ma and Needles are in Baghdad and Dood is in Abu Dhabi. Most Iraqi families are like that now. They have joined the Lebanese and Palestinians who are already well-dispersed across continents. In fact, probably half the world's population is making do or trying to make a living somewhere other than in their native home towns.

Tawadud is dead, Dhafir is dead, and so is Naila's dad. The toll continues.

Nidhal thinks that although one romanticizes one's country when in exile, one can look at it more objectively. I asked her whether she was happy now that she's back in Lebanon. 'Well, yes and no,' she said. 'It may have been easier to be born a Swede, or belong to any democratic country where humans are treated as humans. But as I wasn't, I try to do the best I can within my own. I have made my theatre an open place for dialogue between the public and the actors – between the arts and the real world – because I think that the theatre is the only place where one can perform the thin dividing line between fiction and reality, present and future.' The other night we attended a performance of Camus' *Caligula* at her theatre. It was performed, with full visual horror, violence and sexual overtones, by a young troupe of Syrian actors. The troupe had already performed this play in Damascus. They had been allowed to do so by the Syrian censors, even though it must have been obvious to even the densest of them that this play resonated with comparisons to the political situation they, and we, all live in. So maybe Nidhal does have a point.

In Lebanon, even after seventeen years of civil war, viciously fought by all factions for no rational or fathomable reason, there still is some semblance of free speech left. The right to grumble and complain, a national characteristic, has not been banned. That is why Lebanon has always been the perfect place for political exiles from all over the Arab world to retire to – this was true for our grandfathers' and fathers' generations, as well as our own. One could not wish for a better place of refuge.

Identity

9 June 1996 – Beirut
Ma told us a story of her great-grandmother today. She was from the Iraqi tribe of Delaym, a tiny and ugly woman given as a bride to Rifat Beig, who was serving in the Ottoman army in Iraq. He was tall and good-looking, but never took another wife. She used to make him *dolma*s (usually made by stuffing vegetables), but she made them from parsley leaves as a *mezze* for his *araq*, which he loved to drink. She ground her own herbs for medicines and poultices, and my mother remembers that Bibi Salha would make these into little square shapes and pop them into mouths. She herself had two daughters.

27 July
I had a blackout, fainted flat on my face, broke five teeth, fractured and dislocated the top part of my jaw and broke the right condyle. Twenty-two stitches under my chin; that was twenty days ago. I now know what it's like to have a mouth full of broken teeth, just like in the movies.

23 August
Election fever has hit Lebanon, and they are something else here. Every Tom, Dick and Harry has plastered his photos everywhere. On trees, all the way up the lampposts, walls,

garbage bins – every available space is covered. Hariri's name is even stencilled on the walls. But at least they *have* elections.

No date
Uday is shot and badly injured in Baghdad.

Due to my broken jaw I have to wear a horrid painful brace like a horse's bridle. I do not feel like the most sociable human being right now.

10 March 1997 – London
Baghdad Diaries still not published. I had dinner with Toby, who says he thinks it's political; there are lots of nice remarks about it, but they all say there is no market for it.

14 March – New York
I arrive at JFK. When my turn comes in the queue, I hand in my passport. The lady behind the counter says, 'Ma'am, did they tell you what they do to you when you arrive at this airport'?

'No,' I say, horror written all over my face.

She softens her tone and says, 'Well, it's not that bad'. I am given a red file and sent to an end room. About ten people are there already – Poles, a few Spaniards and an irate Irish boy who wants to break everything. So I try to calm him down. He yells, 'This is racism!'

I tell him, 'No it's democracy; and you Irish are always up to no good, just like us Iraqis.'

'But I have only come for St. Patrick's Day, and why did the lady at the counter not know what that was?'

I say, 'New York is a big place and she might not be a Catholic.' I spent five years in an Irish convent, so I know.

My turn comes; I stand in front of a white sheet, where a Polaroid is taken. Two pictures and two sets of fingerprints; my fingerprints are full of whorls and lines, easy to identify. 'That's good,' the officer there says. The people who worst off are those who work in agriculture – they have nearly no markings from the chemicals they use. I ask him why this did not happen four years ago when I last came through New York. He says, 'you were shooting at us.'

'What do you mean,' I say, '*you* were shooting at *us*!' He looks confused.

Then comes the customs officer: 'When were you last in Iraq?'

'Two years ago,' I say.

'Have you been to Turkey?'

'Why Turkey?' I ask.

'I am asking the questions, not you,' he says aggressively. 'You can ask me when I am finished.'

I ask again, and he says, 'Are you a Kurd?'

I say, 'I have some Kurdish blood; most Iraqis do, we are a very mixed race.'

'Are you Kurdish,' he asks again.

'No,' I say. 'Just some blood.'

'Well you're not,' he decides. It seems that the Kurds are all escaping through the north and into Turkey, so I could have been a runaway Kurd.

15 March

Cannot change a hundred-dollar bill; the subway lady won't take more than a twenty-dollar bill – Q says no one will change a hundred-dollar bill except the university co-op. My frozen bank account in England doesn't allow me to take out my money, let alone have a plastic card. The UK was the only country after the Gulf War to freeze the assets of every Iraqi. They said it was because of the UN sanctions, but that's not true – it's the Brits. I am just an artist with a few thousand dollars in the bank; it's pathetic. I wouldn't even know how to buy a screw for a tank, let alone a weapon of mass destruction.

18 March

This morning I had an appointment with Christine Nelson, the curator of manuscripts at the Morgan Library. They are going to have an exhibition of diaries and mine might be included. At the Morgan Library café, where we met, each table had a vase with yellow freesias in them, and guess what was in my hair– a yellow freesia! It was the first thing she noticed. I owned up to pinching them on occasion for my hair but certainly not today – just a coincidence … It turns out to be a good omen because I am going to be in the exhibition 'Private Histories: Four Centuries of Journal Keeping', which will open on 24 April 1997. I am going to be among the greats like Thoreau, Pepys, and Brontë. What a thrill!

20 March

The paper wastage in the USA is something horrendous. Each morning a ton of junk mail arrives at the door. As for the 'Zion Times', as Sol calls *The New York Times*, it's half a tree's worth of paper that has to be thrown out everyday. I am trying to find a dentist – it's a thousand dollars a tooth. Everyone is insured, so it does not bother them. But what about the uninsured? Another characteristic of the USA: everyone seems to sue everyone else all the time. It's like a national pastime.

Vegetables and fruit have no taste or smell in case someone with an allergy sues. It is all appearances.

One hears more Spanish than English everywhere; I sometimes wonder where I am. South America must be empty.

25 March

Q says the most expert doctor to see my broken jaw is named David Israel – that's a little too much, I will have to keep my broken jaw. Q says most good doctors are Jewish. I say, just as long as he is not a rabid Zionist.

Had this excellent idea today after endless talk of Palestine and Israel. All Palestinians living in Israel should wear a yellow star and stick one on each shop and house they own. They cannot move a centimetre in their own towns and villages without their passes; would the Israelis then realize what they are doing?

2 April – Washington
Ma, Sol and I go to get a new passport for Kiko at the Iraqi Embassy. We come out with new passports for all three of us. Most extraordinary, no hassle – they needed the money. The embassy was like a morgue.

8 April
Q has this brown spotted jacket that Sol hates. Q says, 'but it's Missoni, and it's my favourite.'

Sol says, 'It's twenty years old!'

'Well,' I add, 'it's a little small.'

Sol says it looks like vomit; Q tells her she must never have seen vomit to say that. I say, perhaps dried vomit; and so it goes. Ma later says perhaps Q could give her the jacket for her to turn it into a cushion.

Ma has just heard that Madeleine Albright said that if the USA doesn't sign the treaty against chemical weapons, it will be listed in the same bracket as Iraq and Libya.

26 April
I am writing this aboard the plane on my way to Chicago. When they saw my passport at the airport in New York, a horror-stricken lady escorted me to the checking area, where everything had to be X-rayed. My bags had to be emptied, searched and X-rayed again. Then I was told to pack them up. Everyone was very polite and nice about it. Government policy, they said. Only then was I allowed to board the plane.

In contrast, there I am with the greats at the Morgan Library, my manuscript in a glass showcase with Walt Whitman's under the heading 'War'.

In the exhibition a blown-up statement of mine says 'So many more people have to die and for what? Who the hell wanted Kuwait anyway?' At the entrance to the exhibition a large plaque says, 'FROM ISAAC NEWTON TO NUHA AL-RADI: FOUR HUNDRED YEARS OF DIARY KEEPING.' I nearly had a heart attack when I saw that. Undoubtedly, this is the highest peak I will reach in my life; it could be downhill all the way after this. So there I am, keeping the highest company and the next minute I am a would-be criminal. Can I understand the USA? Why did they give me a visa?

25 July – New York
Went round the Statue of Liberty in a boat – she is a very large lady, not a fashionable anorexic New Yorker.

August – Beirut
Hope seems to have vanished for the Iraqi people. Reality becomes worse by the day. We are being depleted like the depleted uranium used on us. Perhaps that is their ultimate aim. Oil does not contaminate. After all, that's what this whole issue is about, oil and more oil; but it's the Iraqi people who have borne the brunt of it – the war, the embargo, the thousands who die every month from the lack of nutrition, medicine and the pollution of war.

3 January 1998 – Abu Dhabi
I've been a month with Dood and family working for my exhibition at the cultural centre. Today I went to the framer's in the pouring rain. He is a Pakistani. He told me that in his old house where he had lived earlier in the seventies, it used to rain and the water would pour in from the roof and from the road into the house; when he called the landlord to complain, he

answered that he would raise the rent to 600 *dirhams* instead of 400, because now they had water in the house!

27 January
Since the Italians told the cultural centre they were bringing an exhibition of Leonardo da Vinci's work, they have totally forgotten about me. I thought I was going to be in the same monthly programme as Leonardo, but no, not a mention. Their heads are completely turned and all they are getting are plaster casts and maquettes of the wooden machines he invented, plus some photos. Needless to say, Mona Lisa is on the cover of the pamphlet. They have changed my exhibition date as they were on the same day, and they thought no one would attend my exhibition. Someone unknowingly sent an air ticket for Leonardo; perhaps he could come out of his grave and attend the opening!

I had two deliveries of camel bones. I had asked for some from friends who go out into the desert, to use for my recycled sculpture – but they are not as good as the beautiful sun bleached shark fin bones that I found by the sea. The seashore is full of wood, debris washed up; poor trees.

28 January
Fax from Toby – Saqi is going to publish my diary sometime in autumn – whoopee!

9 February
Tons of people came to my exhibition, and Leonardo's is empty. They are bewildered with what they got – no Mona Lisa. (I remember when I first saw her in 1960, I thought, 'what a small thing to be so notoriously famous.' But then the trick is the look in her eyes.)

2 March
Am writing this in Abu Dhabi Airport. There is a story about
how the legal system works in this country. A foreign woman
was hit by a car; during the trial in court the judge said, 'You
are over fifty, of no use any more ... You are not a Muslim ...
Your life is over, so you get no compensation.' She didn't sue
because she knew it would be no use. Legal rights for women
and/or foreigners are practically non-existent here . Only the
natives have rights.

8 June –Amman
As I have a residence permit in Jordan, this is where I get my
visas. It is a lot easier with a residence. Got the USA's the same
day, but the Brits have new rules for Iraqis – one to two months
wait. They tell me it's a go, but slow; and the permission has to
come from the UK.

21 July – New York
Sailed through New York customs this time – perhaps because
I had come from England and not from the Muddled East.

24 August
The USA has exonerated itself of the bombing in Sudan by
saying that Iraq has helped them make the VX in those
supposed factories they hit, so I suppose now Iraq is going to be
bombed again.

October
There was the book launch at Saqi's in London. Tim Llewellyn
introduced me, and I read extracts from the book. Lots of
people came, including two British ex-ambassadors; it was
great, and later we had a party.

17 November

Ma and Needles went back to Baghdad a week ago and I just don't believe what is happening. It seems we can make bombs in a second, we are so brilliant. How we can get all the raw materials for making all these 'weapons of mass destruction' when everyone is watching and the satellites are spying away? It is beyond me. The government has accused some of the inspectors of being spies. It seems they have put listening devices everywhere, and they know where Saddam can be at any given moment.

Clinton will hit, without a doubt.

I am working on a series of Iraqi paintings just in case the Institut du Monde Arabe in Paris gives us an exhibition next year. It helps to be working for a cause right now – there is little else one can do.

Just talked to Ma: Salvi is dead. She didn't want to tell me. There is another dog now.

It seems all they do in Baghdad is go to funerals and console those who have lost families in their absence.

The Americans and Brits are determined to hit. They have some new weapons to try out. *The Sunday Times* says that Israel is working on a new virus that can only get at Arabs. They don't give the name of the scientist.

17 December

The Observer of London has just published a piece they asked me to do in the style of my diary about the bombing in Baghdad. Here it is:

17 DECEMBER 1998: Well, the scenario repeats itself. It could be 17 January 1991. Has time stood still? Stayed up all night with CNN. I knew it was coming; with only a few days to Ramadan, it just had to be now. Little did I realize when I wrote my diary in Baghdad in '91 that I would be watching

the bombing of my city on CNN in Beirut eight years later. 'Live,' they keep saying, but it's not. It's quite different. There is no danger; you can lower the volume, switch it off. It's safe, just a realistic made-for-TV movie. It gives no idea of the scale of its actual fright, of the enormity of war.

What really irritates me is that they keep talking and worrying about their boys, brave soldiers, how to protect them. Never mind that they are bombing people on the ground.

Clinton looks straight into the cameras, tries to look candid, and lies. Just how are we threatening America exactly, and why is it in danger? Blair has become poker-faced and shifty. We did not get an up-to-date picture of Saddam, so I can't compare.

Out of 500 UN supervision visits, five were contested. Is that fair? We have to be bombed for that? I'm not so sure Saddam didn't want the bombing, either. It breaks the stalemate: the embargo is not likely to be lifted. Clinton, it suits, but I just can't make out what Blair thinks he is doing. The telephone hasn't stopped ringing since 7 a.m. At least people care.

It's now 2 p.m. Have finally got through to Ma in Bags. She said the house shook a lot and it was very loud. She and Needles just sat in the hall and drank herbal tea. She said they had been out to dinner that night: 500 ladies at the Alwiyah Club. She told Dood on the phone that morning that Iraqi women are tough as old boots ... forgot to ask her if they got home before the air raid.

CNN says 70 percent of Americans approve of the bombing. Are they sick or something, these Americans? I wish someone would bomb them at home. As that's not likely we'll have to settle for a few natural disasters. Let's hope another hurricane hits them and devastates half their land. I can't believe how callously they talk. They calmly give times for when they are going to bomb. And even the places they bomb are full of UN cameras monitoring. These supposed weapons of mass destruction. Hidden away. Secret. Underground. Surely they must be rusted by now. We have a very harsh climate.

Now it's 11 p.m. and I have dragged my mattress into the sitting room because I had a very uncomfortable night last night on the sofa. Why do they keep giving us desert names: Desert Storm, Desert Fox? We are actually the Fertile Crescent.

Christiane Amanpour on CNN says: 'The noise is so loud, can you hear me?' It's what never leaves me, the noise, 'til now.

Why are we singled out for special punishment? And a worse punishment than the bombs would be to have that lethal man Butler return to Iraq. I really cannot understand how we could still be such a threat to the world. Look at Israel: it bombs the south of Lebanon constantly; it breaks the sound barrier over Beirut nearly daily, it occupies Lebanese land. Tell me, are they not the aggressors?

We are very alone now, but may we remain fertile like the Crescent that is our identity in so many ways. There is no quick fix to the Iraqi problem. I know we are an easy target. I know we are a thorn in everyone's flesh. But I feel very, very sad, because we are also a people.

19 December
Third night in front of the TV on my mattress – it's Ramadan. Will they continue bombing? Managed to get through to Ma again. She says they call the trio of Butler, Blair and Clinton 'the BBC'.

20 December
The USA has just said bombing is off, four days have achieved their objective.

325 Tomahawks

90 Cruise Missiles

About a hundred important sites bombed.

In Baghdad today there was a funeral for 68 people.

The UNSCOM mission is over. Butler took everyone out the night before the bombing. And Baghdad says 'No more spies, they have bombed everything anyway.'

UNSCOM have spent all these years installing expensive cameras and listening devices at all the sites they thought could be used for war production, naturally paid for by Iraqi money. Then they bombed all the places they had put them in! What was the point of the whole exercise?

CNN says they lobbed the last few cruise missiles into Baghdad. I ask you. They think they are playing baseball. Nazar Hamdoun says that Butler fixed the whole thing with the American administration so that they could bomb Iraq. It seems Scott Ritter said that too last week. Butler was looking even more shifty than usual. He is a real snake in the grass, and no offence to snakes. Clinton calls Saddam 'an enemy of peace' – what does that make the USA and UK after this – just friendly fire and collateral damage!? Those are favourite descriptions used by the USA when a mistake occurs and innocent people die.

There is so much news going on, one doesn't know what to follow between the Clinton impeachment, the Iraq war and the parliament in Lebanon where everyone is accusing the other of thievery.

23 December

The USA bought 3.6 million barrels of oil from Iraq during this crisis. Then they bombed the Basra refinery. Now they say they will allow Iraq to produce more oil, because the oil price is down and there is not enough money to pay for the UN oil-for-food programme, but we cannot produce more because our refineries need extensive repair. We cannot get permission to make repairs because the parts needed could be used for weapons of mass destruction. How magnanimous of the USA to permit this impossibility.

24 December
The USA reserves the right to bomb Iraq again; Sandy Berger says they will bomb the minute Saddam starts his weapons industry. What are they talking about? Was there any response from the Iraqi side? Was there even a whiff of chemical or poison gas in the air after all their bombings on supposed dangerous sites?

26 December
The Iraqi's called Operation Desert Fox 'Operation Monica'.

31 December
I am spending New Year's with Minni, Yahya and family in the Deir al-Kamar Monastery of the Moon. The moon is really big here and looms large overhead.

2 January 1999
We have told the UN that we are afraid we cannot vouchsafe the security of American or British nationals. They will have to send other nationalities for their inspectors.

6 January
I have a horrible feeling we are going to be hit again. Clinton is cornered and he has promised a sudden attack on us because we are flying in our own skies. What the strong and the brave do: press buttons from far away.

8 January
Butler is thinking of resigning. Would that that could be true – one horror less.

The Israelis continue to bomb South Lebanon and break the sound barrier over our heads in Beirut. I don't think the window panes can take much more.

Scott Ritter says the whole of UNSCOM was organised to spy on the Iraqi government and had nothing to do with the development of the arms industry. The Arabs are in a complete tangle now – they didn't need anything else to tangle them, because for once they teamed up together against Iraq and got fooled. A friend says the Arab leaders live on borrowed security. They pay the USA to stay in power and able to remain on their various thrones. They probably don't even receive all the armaments they have to buy, paying an exorbitant price.

11 January
Phoned Ma last night. She said, 'Pray for us.' Iraq did not accept the 1991 Kuwait boundaries, so we are back to Square One. Are we just going to be bombed out of existence?

Meanwhile, Israel is happily bombing away in South Lebanon.

Samir was just saying, why can't we do something that relates to us? Why does everything have to come from the West?

'How far back do you want to go,' I asked. 'The Middle East is at the crossroads between East and West, with five hundred years of Ottoman rule followed by various colonial powers dividing and cutting us into bits in the twentieth century. Is it any wonder that we have managed to lose our identity? '

14 January
Outlook Programme on the BBC says 300 tons of depleted uranium in the southern battle area in Iraq are causing horrendous defects, babies with no heads, no eyes – there are no computers to make an exact count. It has seeped through the earth into the water system, which means agriculture is also affected. What is on the ground can still be cleaned, but it's a very expensive exercise. What is in the air remains in the air

blowing around. So it's a catastrophe for centuries to come. Hiroshima is still paying for its bombardment and we are far worse off. Both are victims of American technology. All the US soldiers who took part in the Gulf War, and who had shrapnel wounds, still show depleted uranium in their sperm. In the 250 'Gulf families', 60 percent of children have been born with congenital defects. So what of Iraq?

21 January
Clinton is backing seven groups of Iraqi opposition living in the West. What kind of standard is that? Talk about not putting all your eggs in one basket.

There was a wonderful translation on one of the Lebanese TV stations the other day from a French programme: 'Cézanne' was literally translated into Arabic as 'sixteen donkeys' [*seize ânes*].

26 January
The USA says it's Saddam's fault that the missile went wrong and hit a lot of poor people ... they are now hitting targets in the north near Mosul.

The latest with the USA is that it is threatening Europe with sanctions, because of the banana boycott. Would that it would happen, so that they could feel what sanctions do.

King Hussein has been rushed back to the USA, low blood count. Not good news. Abdullah, King in a day.

5 February
Gosh, amazing, all of a sudden no more King Hussein.

10 February
Kiko has had a really bad accident. A friend of his backed into him in his lorry, smashed his leg: lots of blood, kneecap popped

out. He had a big operation, but he is able to walk. Can talk to him on Sunday; Sol has flown over to see him.

In Amman, two palaces are open to the public to receive condolences. He was a mighty king in the old sense of the word.

13 February

Went to Tyre yesterday, a tragedy of Israeli bombing. All those beautiful houses on the seafront were bombed. We couldn't see them, but we could hear the bombing going on inland. The local fishermen are only allowed to fish close to the shore; the minute they venture out a little, they get caught by the Israeli patrol – it seems they want all the fish too.

16 February

Forty-two air raids on Iraq yesterday. That's war.

What hypocrisy! How could the Kurds be terrorists on the Turkish side of the border and have a safety zone to protect them on the Iraqi side? The USA invites the two Iraqi Kurdish factions, the Talibani and Barzani clans, for peace negotiations. Then the CIA, with the help of Mossad, trap Ocalan, the leader of the Turkish Kurds, and send him back to Turkey as a bribe so as to use Ingerlik, the Turkish airbase, to bomb Iraq – their favourite occupation. Brute force is the only method the USA knows; after all, it conquered America by killing nine tenths of its native population. Now it seems that fate awaits the rest of the world.

1 March

Six thousand children die every month in Iraq: a UNICEF statistic, attributable to the UN embargo. The embargo has killed more people than any mass destruction weapon. This is all done under the eyes and the conscious knowledge of the world. Where are the human rights the UN stands for?

About 2000 wonderful students marched into Arnoun, a border town in Lebanon occupied by the Israelis, and cut through the barbed wire and freed the town. I phoned up Minni to say what wonderful news and she says Kamal (her son) was one of the liberators. He had been late coming home, and she was ready to give him a piece of her mind when he told her. She sat him down, brought out her video camera, said, 'now speak' and recorded him, LIVE.

In Iraq the air raids are non-stop, and we have turned down the inspectors.

6 March

I love the banana war. It's getting serious, and now the Italians are also outraged at the American pilot who severed the *téléferique* wire, killing all those people. All the earlier complaints that the planes were always flying too low went unheeded . The pilot got away with nothing; the Americans had tried him in the USA and said the machine was faulty.

Today Rifat told us a story of his prison time in Baghdad. He asked the chap beside him what he was in for. He answered, 'I dreamed one night that there had been a coup, and Ahmed Hassan Bakr was killed. So the next day he related his dream at the office, a security chap reported it and there he was in jail!

10 March

Went with Nabil, my lawyer, to see what had happened to my residence permit. He said they were going slow because a lot of bribery was going on. Now no bribery is allowed, we have this new clean government, so they only have their salaries to live on – hence the protest. There were a couple of large chaps sitting behind desks throwing paper clips at each other. I still don't know anything about my permit.

31 March

Yet another horrible interview for my residence permit and I might soon have to have another. It's the dreaded Iraqi passport.

3 April

We are out of the limelight now due to the Kosovo crisis. What is it in the Balkans that makes for constant turmoil? It will not finish with the bombing because they have not solved the Bosnian refugee question yet. Thousands have nowhere to go. Is this World War III? I hate this no-hope situation and I feel for everyone all around.

23 April

It's amazing, the similarity in people's behaviour. The Serbians are saying the same thing as us: why are you hurting the people? And the USA says, we have nothing against Iraqi or Serb people –its Saddam and Milosevic. But it's the ordinary people who suffer and have nowhere to go. It's the infrastructure – the essence of a country – that gets it, every time.

26 April

They have started worrying about who will pay for the Serbian bombing. For continuity we are getting bombed too – lest anyone forget Iraq.

Ma says when a baby girl was born in the old days they would collect a whole pile of ant eggs and rub it on her body so she would be hairless. I said, 'I wish you had done it to me.' My cyber-café has been hit by a virus. 'Come back tomorrow,' they say.

27 April

It is called 'the Chernobyl virus'. Came back home and heard on the radio that Turkey has been hit by it too.

28 April
I was just listening to the radio about Salvador Dalì's brother; it seems he had been manufacturing a whole lot of Dalì fakes and has just been taken in for questioning. I go downstairs and our grocer, Abu El-Izz calls me in and asks, could I give him a bit of advice. A friend of his had just called and said he had a painting by Salvador Dalì.

'He says it is worth a million.'

'Don't touch it with a ten-foot barge pole', say I.

'But it has a signature', he says.

'So does a forgery', I reply. He couldn't take it in and felt disappointed at the loss of this prospective fortune. He said he would show me a photo. It's a painting all about space stuff. I love coincidences like that.

16 May
We have a nightingale visiting us – what a sound. Birds don't know when to sleep nowadays, because the Saudi Embassy has its floodlights on full blast, all night. Though they seem to have flourished and increased by hundreds. I have sparrows, *bulbul*s and doves. I feed them on my balcony. The nightingale is still singing.

4 June
Went for the residence permit again today. Fingerprints are now required, and we still have to go again. I am totally depressed. How many more months do I have to wait for it to finish?

17 June
My residence was refused. It's been five months now of waiting. My horrid, lying lawyer just took money from me. I feel so low. But I am going down with Suha to drink mint tea by the sea.

24 June

Nidal phoned and said that she was working like six donkeys and six mules. Good, I said, we have all got to work like donkeys – we might hit the jackpot like the one in Egypt, which made a big sensation recently. A donkey walking in the desert fell into a hole, and they found hundreds of mummies, gold, etc. It seems they had been looking for this site for years.

No news on the residence-permit front. Nidal promises to look into it.

25 June

At the Goethe Institute, we are listening to a lecture when the lights go out. Generator starts – we leave later for a friend's house next door. I said it's the Israelis – everyone boohooed me. Coming back home, the whole of Beirut is in pitch darkness except for a few generators working. My landlord took me up the stairs with his flashlight. He said it was the Israelis. After that, it was another wonderful musical night, with Israeli jets coming overhead, breaking the sound barrier, and the Lebanese firing whatever they have in defence.

Christina phoned her broadcasting station in Germany to ask if she could send them something about the situation. They said, 'It's okay, we have a correspondent in Tel Aviv.'

'But Israel is bombing Lebanon – what about this side?'

They hemmed and hawed, and in the end said, 'We have no money.'

Seems a lot of damage has been done to the electricity station and many bridges have been hit.

26 June

Everyone is very depressed, they cannot face starting all over again. The civil war is still very fresh in people's minds. Saudi Arabia and Iran say they will help to rebuild.

Regardless of the dire situation, in the evening the European Beauty Contest pageant held in Beirut went ahead!

Rima phoned to say I am going to be invited to this Medécins sans Frontières event in Dubai. It is to be the longest painting in the world: ten kilometres, to be painted in a day so it can get into the Guinness Book of Records.

27 June
Ma said, 'I lit a candle for you yesterday at the Kiddass.' So I say,
'Sol has lit candles in the whole of France for my residence.'
I live in fear and trepidation, but am going down to the sea for a swim anyway.

29 June
The streets are in blocks of light or darkness, depending on which section of Beirut has electricity. The house is shaking from the sound of generators; the downstairs one has a deafening roar while the upstairs one shakes the whole house. Generators are the most anti-social machines, just noise and dirt polluters.

It is the season of kittens. Lebanon, I think, is a cat country, as opposed to Iraq being more dog. Magda goes round with contraceptive pills trying to keep the population down.

Tomorrow is residence permit day again, I feel a bit sick.

7 July
Since we went to see the Ayurvedic doctor, the kitchen has been lined with bottles of brown liquids: one for taking off moles, another for digestion and well-being, etc. It is difficult to decide which horror to start the day with. Ma says her moles are dropping off at the rate of knots. I have written to Q about this herb *talool*. I have asked around, and we think it's St.John's Wort in English. Maybe it can cure cancer; after all, a mole is a growth too.

Our electricity cuts are really bad.

2 August
Beginning of the 10th anniversary of the UN embargo. Will it ever be lifted? One day when Iraq is not the pariah of the world, perhaps the injustice – now to the scale of genocide – will have to be answered for. But sadly, it will be too late for all those who have died

11 August
Waiting for the total eclipse. Everyone has gone crazy with terror, expecting the end of the world.

15 August
It was not that exciting, only 82% so not a total eclipse for us. The paranoia was extreme; people bolted themselves inside their houses with all shutters shut and sat terrified at home. I saw it through an old X-ray of my back.

20 August
Ma's latest medical cure: she wraps her knee with a piece of cabbage and sleeps all night with it – an old cure, she says. What do you do with the cabbage leaf next day, I ask her, as Ma is a natural-born recycler. She said, 'I throw it on the hillside for the chickens.' I heave a sigh of relief.

Amal, the director of my art gallery, came to see my artwork today to see what she had let herself in for, but she liked what I had done and laughed and said people were fed up with the norm. I have a whole series of paintings dealing with cell phones.

My residence permit has been refused yet again.

10 September
Went to Deir al-Kamar with Minni to watch Shahla make fig jam. Shahla is a fount of information about old traditions. In the old days, she said, three months before Christmas, each family would get a sheep or two depending on the size of the

family. They would tie it up and feed it three times a day with mulberry leaves stuffed with silkworm droppings, which is only mulberry leaf concentrate. At the end there would be a competition to see whose sheep was fattest. Another trick for last-minute fattening was to give it salt, which would make the sheep drink a lot of water. The sheep would get so fat that they would have stretch marks like a pregnant woman. Most of the meat would be preserved, so that it could be eaten during the year.

29 September
Between Nidal and Yahya's string-pulling I am now sitting in the office of the head of security, the big boss. There is hope; his second in command is a lady also named Nuha. I am to come back Friday for a final decision.

No date
Got it in one hour! I cannot believe it, after seven months of jagged nerves and hysteria a miracle. Open sesame, thanks to my friends.

28 October
Nearly the end of my exhibition, have not done too well but am doing the stage props for Nidal's new play, an Arabic version of *Three Tall Women* by Edward Albee. Such fun. There is a multi-story, unfinished building from wartime Beirut in front of the theatre, a huge space, so I am working on the third floor in the open. It is full of dirt ,empty bottles and spent bullets. I am painting seven metres of sea and sky.

2 November – Dubai
I am in Dubai for the longest painting in the world, and am staying at this plush hotel with highly polished marble crawling up the walls – but in the bathroom, a rude sign says 'if you want

a souvenir you can buy any of these items in the shop downstairs'.

Petra, the organiser, says 'Please, please, you have to paint at least ten metres.' We have to dress for dinner and go out for this big 'do in tents, one hour deep in the desert. Robert Rauschenberg is our biggest star. What excitement.

4 November

At eight in the morning we meet downstairs. A taxi is waiting; there is a wind blowing. Oh! Oh! We get to the site, miles of cars already there. Fifty schools have been invited to participate, and some had already started. With horror, we saw that the wind had blown the canvas that had been neatly laid out in great tangles all over the road and desert. Our stop was at Kilometre 5. We get there and begin, but the wind is blowing everything away. Have to sit on the canvas. A German artist wearing a super boiler suit outfit with kneepads is beside me. She is dancing while throwing and dripping the paint: a Pollock! The press are thrilled with her. Meanwhile all are having interviews in the sandstorm. The whole thing is quite unreal. At eleven, we are told to pack up and go, as it is raging by now. After lunch we artists are taken to a large hall, where we continued to paint. It was great. By the end I had done 25 metres.

5 November

I can hardly move from all that activity yesterday. Everything feels sore. Medécins Sans Frontières' efforts to bring the world together and make the world's longest painting – a picture of hope for children – did not succeed. They wanted to show art as an international medium that has no borders. But nature has a funny way of answering such impossible ventures, and brought us a sandstorm that blew away our hopes.

6 November
Have read 'Diary of a Political Idiot' in *Granta*. The writer is Serbian; it's far more literary and poetic than mine, but there are many similarities. I wonder if she had read mine. They are also political prisoners of their leader. I really wish the USA could get some of its own medicine. They are so reluctant to have body bags come home but have no thought of the body bags they are inflicting on others. These modern wars, Vietnam, Kosovo, us, are too big to handle by the human beings on the receiving side. They are totally devastating.

10 November
Got caught in a downpour today and totally drenched. I took shelter in a nearby shop. A chap standing beside me asked,
    'Do you know what is happy and revived?
    'What?'
    'The flower in your hair,' he said. We laughed and had a chat. Rain doesn't seem to want to stop. It is a compulsive habit to always have a flower in my hair.

16 December–14 January 2000
We are spending New Year's 2000 at Dood's house, 'l'Averina', in Tuscany: a family get-together. Solstice night on the 22nd, and the moon was shining like a beacon. It's the closest it's been to Earth this century.
    For New Year's we have thirty people for dinner, and there are fireworks in the town across the valley from us. Beautiful sky, but very cold. I've had five of those dreaded scorpions in the house 'til now, and we have had the usual family squabbles.

20 January 2000 – Beirut
A storm has been raging now for two days. It takes small breaks and starts up again, winds of up to 60 mph, waves 10 metres high, floods everywhere. And today of all days they have come

to change the electricity in our building from 110 to 220 volts. Cranes and huge transformers are parked outside in the raging wind. The ground floor ladies had a huge drama around 7 p.m. – their boiler burst and went up in much smoke, lots of screaming. It's always like an Egyptian movie down there.

Since we have had our 220 volts, there have been nothing but dramas. For Ma's farewell dinner last night, the electricity disappeared in the afternoon and all the cooking and dinner had to be done by candlelight. All the guests were given some rhubarb root to take home. It eases the nerves, helps constipation, cleans the blood and so on, according to our Ayurvedic doctor. Electricity didn't come back 'til ten this morning, whereupon shrieks and puffs of smoke emerge and waft up into our living room from the ground-floor ladies.

The crazy storm is still with us, it's now nearly a week.

5 February

I have made contact with Jasmina, what fun. she wrote the Serbian diary. I had sent her a letter c/o *Granta* and just got an e-mail back. I want to start an anti-war group. She, it seems, is a feminist in Belgrade; I have never been inclined towards segregation. It exists in such a large sphere in our society socially that I don't think it's the answer, after all it's men who make war – so what is the point of a bunch of women being pacifists? This new anti-war group must have no gender, colour or creed limits.

What is happening in Chechnya is just horrific. I am sure Russia has been allowed to get away with doing all this in Chechnya so that the USA could do what they like in Iraq.

7 February

Bombed again, this time worse than in June. I was woken up by the sound of the jets, but as it is quite a normal happening, I had passed out again. The electricity stations in Beirut, Tripoli and Baalbek have been hit. Iraq invaded Kuwait for six months, was defeated and left, and is still being bombed on a daily basis for it. Israel invaded Jordan, Syria, Lebanon and let's not forget Palestine – it seems like centuries ago. They don't move out and feel it is their due right to bomb. They don't get 'sanctioned' – just a pat on the back, and commiserated with: poor Israel is just trying to survive. What a lot of bull this Western justice is.

Went out and bought a rechargeable lantern. Came back to see it's made in China with instructions saying do not put into fire – what could that mean?

9 February
I bet Barak bombed Lebanon like Clinton bombed Iraq, whenever he was in a political jam. Israel has all its corruption scandals going on.

Sol and Dood phoned to ask how things are. I said I am so used to it I just switch into automatic. We have been rigged to a building opposite that has a generator and we get 5 amps each; it's a small generator. They say we might get electricity back by May.

11 February
Cess is back from the USA. He says he didn't know the electricity situation was so bad. They don't write the doings of Israel in the US papers.

Magda gave me a Chinese fortune cookie today. It said, 'Anyone has talent at twenty-five. Try having it at fifty.' I am afraid I am heading in that direction, long past fifty. Time is up.

16 February
Today, not only has the head of the UN, Hans Von Sponek, resigned in Baghdad, so has Utta Berkhart at the WFO – because they feel sanctions are only harming the people and not affecting the authorities. Dennis Halliday had resigned a couple of years earlier for the same reasons. The USA said they were

relieved by the resignations because they had gone against their wishes. Imagine that!

Our electricity is functioning miraculously, with only short cuts.

It's pouring rain with huge winds again, and my inspiration has totally vanished since Magda gave me that Chinese cookie. How am I going to earn a living?

Told Jasmina today if more people knew people like her they would stop thinking Milosevic *is* Serbia. And if more people knew people like me they would stop thinking Saddam *is* Iraq.

I have one female and six male cats, and it's February and there is pandemonium on my balcony.

18 February

The big student demonstrations in Beirut managed to get on BBC English radio. They are objecting to the USA, saying it's all Hizbullah's fault – Hizbullah are becoming the heroes of the day.

29 February – Leap Year

Angela Flowers on the BBC says today is the day when ladies propose to men. Got an interesting piece of information from Bert today: the Medicis made their money through drugs and medicine, and that's where the name come from. *Medici* – from *medico* – is plural for 'doctors'.

3 March

I am now waiting for a Cypriot visa. I am supposed to have an exhibition in Nicosia, but the usual excuses – I wait.

Amir Abdullah of Saudi Arabia is here and has given millions to help with the electricity.

11 March

Still no sign of my visa. Jasmina and I are going to write about 'the globalization of evil' – the title is her idea. She is compiling our letters and wants to publish them one day. Serbia and Iraq, war and embargo.

The most exciting offer I have had is from Sol, who has arranged for me to work as assistant to her master plasterer for her mosque in Yemen in October.

The Arab foreign ministers are very pleased with themselves to be meeting here. No one will solve anything, I am sure. Everyone will just talk about their own problems and go away. Still, it is good for Lebanon.

12 March
The Arab foreign ministers did not even manage to stick it out for two days. We are a sad lot.

It seems Cyprus doesn't give visas to Iraqis – only if you are selling barrels of oil. But if you get washed up on shore, you are taken to prison for three months and after that you are allowed to stay. Well, I think I will give it a miss. The exhibition has to take place without me.

What gives the USA and the UK the right to bomb Iraq every day, and what gives Israel the right to bomb Lebanon every day?

22 March
My poor cats – they are certainly the worse for wear. It's cat time again. My only female has vanished and the motley crew of chaps are doing it to each other. Battle signs show on them: an eye missing here, a leg there.

30 March
Jasmina wrote to say they were celebrating the NATO defeat as a victory. I told her nothing is new. We celebrate all our defeats. It's a dictatorship trait.

22 April

How could we Arabs be such a useless bunch of people? The Arabs are silent. It is only Hizbullah that does anything. Israel is going to withdraw in a couple of months from the south of Lebanon. But will anything survive 'til then, with all the non-stop bombing that's going on?

Uday has been voted 'Journalist of the Century' in Baghdad by 97% according to Radio Monte Carlo.

Phoned Ma this morning. They are battling with termites in the house again.

4 May

A new supermarket has opened near us. We only have three others within a couple of hundred metres of each other. Huge traffic jams – it is an event. In the dire financial straits that Lebanon is in, the only thing that seems to work is food and more food. Finally I went in yesterday, thought I would buy some ham. The guy behind the counter yelled at me: 'It's pig! Pig!' I said yes – he was utterly horrified, but finally started slicing some. I didn't dare tell him I was a pig-eating Muslim. The supermarket is underground.

25 May

National Liberation Day.

The occupied south has been liberated and Michael has come to report on it, so I am joining her to go down south in her taxi. We started in Naqqura; the area looks like a miniature White Cliffs of Dover. It is the UN outpost in Lebanon. Michael went in to see Timur Koksal, or Timur the Turk, as the chief is called.

I sat in the poet's café. Its owner came 14 years ago; their houses had been burnt by the Israelis. They took up this post and contracted to feed the UN. Journalists are pouring in. We are going to go along the whole Lebanese-Israeli border, along the newly liberated towns. We saw burnt-out tanks.

Palestine is so visible across the barbed wire. People were standing in rows and rows just looking across, through the barbed wire demarcation line. The other side was very subdued, just a few cars every now and then, their villages or kibbutzes all identical, same very neat boxlike houses with red roofs.

We had lunch at the UN Indian Battalion group. It consisted of two women, the doctor, the nurse and 550 men. They have clinics and treat the geriatrics in the area, as those are who have remained behind all this time. Going back took seven hours of traffic jams, but no one was complaining. No army, no guns: this could never have happened anywhere else in the Arab world. There isn't that kind of paranoia in Lebanon. After twenty-two years of occupation, the whole country is here and celebrating; it's wonderful. Hizbullah are the heroes of the day. There were banners everywhere saying, 'Thank you Hizbullah', signed by all the liberated towns.

11 June
Ma is in between romance novels and the making of three gallons of apricot sherbet.

12 June
Hafiz Assad is dead: 'The Lion Next Door'. (I wrote that to Handy and Jasmina, and they both thought I was living near a zoo.) 'Lion' in Arabic is *assad*. The whole of Beirut was shut yesterday – a ghost town. Every body was watching TV.

27 June
It seems Kissinger has to telephone and ask the Pentagon if it is safe for him to leave whenever he wants to travel to Europe now, after the Pinochet issue.

17 September
A new law in Baghdad: the euro is going to be the new currency for all foreign transactions. What a wonderful idea. I am all for strengthening Europe. Ma says maybe it's advice from the French. They have a huge frozen stash of our dollars. I, too, am going to open a euro account.

22 September
Thanks to Nidal I am now waiting for the renewal of my residence permit for this year. Am treated royally, but fear still grips with the memory of last year's agony.

6 October
Beirut airport is full of businessmen talking on their cell phones making last-minute deals. How did the world function before cellular phones? 'BC' gets a new meaning now.

8 October – Amman
Just came for two days to clock in for my residence permit here. I am on my way to Yemen. When I reach the passport checking area, the passport-control chap says,
   'All residence permits issued by the Palace have to have an accompanying letter permitting them to travel.'
   Histrionics are to no avail: security men are cold fish. I naturally miss my plane. At five o'clock just when Sol would be waiting to pick me up at the airport in Sana'a, I am here at the Amman airport waiting for Freako to arrive. She doesn't, but it is our fault. Her plane is tomorrow. So there are no-shows both at Sana'a and at Amman – what a coincidence. Nazha says it's voodoo. It seems the new law is due to one Filipino Palace worker who skipped the country. That's why everyone now needs a letter. That's why they kept asking me, 'What do you work as in the Palace?' I said I didn't, I just got the residence permit through friends and I've had it for ten years.

News from Baghdad – we heard that 80 pimps and prostitutes have been executed. Naila says now all pimps and prostitutes can ask for legitimate political asylum.

11 October – Sana'a
Sol's flat at AIYS is a charmer. It's a beautiful old house and her quarters are on the top, the sixth floor. It's full of different niches and little windows with alabaster slabs, carved stucco with bits of blue and red glass studded in it, which keeps changing depending on the light. The telephone rings endlessly but does not connect. Later the whole exchange system goes to be mended.

Two fat *bulbul*s on the balcony. I give them some bread. From the bathroom window I see the house next door with a huge TV dish on the roof leaning precariously, under which a whole bunch of white chickens huddle: telecommunications meets the third world. Sol will be here by four in the afternoon.

13 October
I am staying with Lubna, as Sol has gone off again. I woke to an explosion this morning – later we learned it was at the British Embassy. Lubna works for WFP and one of their programmes is for educating girls. Parents get rice and oil at the end of each month if they enrol their daughters in school. It's a very popular programme.

It is Friday and all the *imam*s appear to be in front of microphones ranting and raving.

15 October
A Saudi hijacks a plane to Iraq – what will happen next? No humanity in Saudi Arabia, he says, and is protesting against repression. What about humanity in Iraq? His reason: it is the only country in the Middle East not under US hegemony.

I am happy to see CNN showing a bit of the Palestinian side. I wonder, is that shown in Europe and the USA, or is it just for our consumption? Lubna's house is next door to Yasser Arafat's – it's an ugly house, but fancy him having a house here.

18 October

We are in Rada, where Sol has been working on and off for the last fifteen years on a 16thcentury mosque built by Sultan Amir in 1505. It's a majestic, white-plastered mosque that looks like a great big beautiful wedding cake. I have been working already for two days with Ali, the master plasterer. I am sort of getting the hang of it. Here every second kid is called Saddam; this is very disconcerting. It is not so in Iraq.

Twenty-first-century decoration everywhere in Yemen is plastic bags – black, green, pink – on every tree, barbed wire, barrier or corner. Every day nearly every Yemeni buys a plastic bag's worth of *ghat* (a Yemeni version of cocoa leaves), chews it and throws away the bag. Before nylon they might have wrapped it in cloth or banana leaves which would disintegrate, leaving no litter.

One week later

Sol and I go to work at seven, come back at noon, go again at two and stay 'til four or five in the afternoon. I think I have learned the trade – it has a lot in common with my old ceramic days – but it requires backbreaking positions to work in. The lime kiln was fired yesterday: very exciting, as they chant and work in a chain with great rhythm. It's a very laborious process, this making of *qudad* (a waterproofing material made partly from lime and partly from volcanic dust cinders). In the afternoon most workers chew *ghat*, lounge about and talk. There are lots of weddings, just about every night, with shooting to celebrate. I ask them if they are all related and invited to go to all the weddings. It seems a notice is put up giving time, place, etc, and all are welcome. Unfortunately guns are imperative in Yemen. It's the first prerequisite for any male Yemeni. The noise is tremendous at almost every hour. There is always some *imam* or other ranting from a minaret at full volume – another modern curse, the microphone. I awake at all sorts of hours during a night that seems eternal. Now it's 7 a.m. and all is quiet.

27 October

We went on our first trip today, to Hilla, a pre-Islamic Himyarite site. We started out with two Toyotas and eleven people and we pick up various tribals with Kalashnikovs on the way, each to cover his tribal area 'til we reach our site. It is huge, with lots of black stone and fossil plants and rocks.

Heard lots of gunshots in the distance. By the time we get back to the cars there are more chaps with Kalashnikovs, and everyone is screaming and yelling. They think we are stealing their gold and treasure. Just as quickly everything settles down, and we are passing fruit all around. Everyone is cheerful. Then they invite us to lunch, but we apologize. Many photos are taken. We all left in a pile of dust.

We have two more with Kalashnikovs in the car now, and we can hardly breathe. I cannot see how an excavation is going to take place here, but Sol says it's always like this and in the end it all works out with just a yelling match every now and then. When we left Rada in the morning our original guard was a big chap named Saleh Arafat who used to be in the National Front for the Liberation of South Yemen. At lunch he sat opposite me and I realized he looked amazingly like Michelangelo. Sol says, 'Well he certainly isn't'... Such a fantastic face, but they all have the most horrid teeth from all that *ghat* chewing.

31 October – Sana'a

There is an American lady also staying at the Institute who just came from Jerusalem where she lives. She is a born-again Christian and thinks religion is very important – she is voting for Bush 'because he has religion and is not a liar; the USA needs a good Christian to be President.'

I said, 'What about all the other religions in the USA'? She was silent.

Then she said, 'If he is a good Christian, he will treat everyone okay.'

1 November

The cyber-café here is completely run by Iraqis. First I met Ibtisam, a chemist who used to work at the nuclear center in Iraq. 'How did they let you out,' I asked. She answered that for two years she was not allowed out, but then it was alright. She has been in Sana'a for four years and does computer programming. Then in walks the son of a relative who recognizes me. He is also doing computer programs and has part ownership in the café. Another Iraqi lurks in the back, a poet from Basra. I was given a huge ice cream and not allowed to pay.

Friday

Just had lunch at Marco's. What a beautiful house and a super collection of oil lamps! He is a fixture in Sana'a. Yemeni lunches have intervals where you change the taste in your mouth with a pastry and honey called *bint el-sahn*, then go back to meat and other dishes. One also has to leave stuff on the plate so as not to show greed, and to indicate that one is no longer hungry. What would the nuns say to that? I think chewing *ghat* is the most unattractive feature of Yemen. Marco says it's unique to Yemen and Ethiopia, so it's one of the special things that makes this area different.

9 November
I am having an exhibition at Dar al-Hajar, the old *imam*'s palace built on a rock, one hour out of Sana'a. It will stay there for one week, then transfer to the museum in Sana'a for another week. I hung my etchings on a line held up with clothes peg – it's fun even though the clothesline has drooped a bit now.

11 November
We walked along the ridge above Dar al-Hajar, where there are many archaeological sites, probably dating to the Himyarite Period. The mountains are so amazing in Yemen. It's almost as though they have been cut out with scissors, the outlines all sharp and jagged.

17 Friday
We meet outside the museum. A convoy will go to Ma'rib to attend a ceremony – the handing over by the German team of the excavated Temple of Barran. I tag along with Sol. We go in a great stream of Toyotas snaking through the landscape, the Minister of Culture in the lead car. More strange mountains, black volcanic tops and yellow and white sand dunes lower down. We reach Ma'rib, dump our stuff at the hotel and head straight for Jidran, the French site, with François, the head of the French Centre in Sana'a.

Jidran is an enormous cemetery – round flat stone tombs, each with a long stone tail -thousands of them. But there is trouble again with the *qabili*s (tribes), who were there in full force, not allowing the archaeologists to work. They say if they are not employed on-site, no one can work. The tribesmen have made themselves a sort of *mafraj* on the ground in the shade of their Toyotas and just sit there. More and more keep arriving. The oil refineries, which can be seen dotting the horizon, are another sore point, because they don't employ them either – only foreign experts. François stays the night as a kind of hostage; he signed a paper stating that next time he would hire them.

To get back into the hotel we had to literally wade through an army and the *qabilis* trying to see the Prime Minister, who is also here for the ceremony. Earlier we had had lunch at a wondrously decorated, kitschy restaurant, all hand-painted by an Egyptian who is a teacher in Ma'rib – the ceilings, the walls: every bit was covered; the food was the worst ever. At dinner there was music and Yemeni dancing – only men. They dance with a very straight back and a half-beat rhythm.

Before the opening ceremony the next day we visited the Ma'rib dam, supposedly one of the seven wonders of the world. It is an object lesson to see that the destruction of a dam could cause the destruction of an empire. On seeing the solidity of the remains, of how this dam was built, one is full of admiration for the craftsmanship. Later, I saw the Turkish ambassador to Yemen and told him to go see the Ma'rib Dam. We talked a lot about the fifth dam being built in Turkey on the Euphrates River that will drown so much territory and deprive Iraq of most of the water from the Euphrates. But then Turkey is one of those countries that is allowed to go beyond all international quota systems.

François came back after signing seven agreements!

22 November
Amman airport. I had to spend fourteen hours at the airport because Yemenia decided not to go to Beirut, as there were only two passengers. So I was dumped in Amman. Yemenia would take no responsibility for their action. I don't dare leave the airport in case I have to get another letter from the Palace, so I transit on chairs and wait for the morning. I stood by the escalator in case I saw someone I knew: so far, only Uns, who is off to Paris. Am watching CNN now, drinking a beer and eating a nasty sandwich, also made by an Iraqi. It's made with awful bread – not his fault. Everyone just laughs when I tell

them that Yemenia cancelled. It must be a joke amongst the airlines.

It's 1.30 in the afternoon and I have just met up with Juan and Nabil Tawhala. I usually meet up with Juan because we have our six-monthly visit to Jordan for our residence permits. We always seem to coincide. Anyway, Nabil says he works for the Hunt Oil Company, so he's been to Ma'rib. He has never managed to see the ruins there because he is afraid of being kidnapped. I say, 'But you are an Iraqi; no one will kidnap you.' He says he is Iraqi but he is also Hunt, which means they can extract something for him – so he always goes by helicopter. Sol spends all her time yelling out the window of her car, 'We are Iraqi!' and we sail through all checkpoints. In Yemen they love us.

22 November – Beirut
Coming back from the airport I get a randy taxi driver who said he loves Iraqi women. 'They have feeling,' he stated. So I tell him I am happily married and have three kids. He says he has seven kids and adds, 'I can't help it. I just love the gals.'

10 December
Am in the air again going to New York and then Mexico and Honduras to visit Kiko. I have another horrid time at Amman airport. This time I have a dual-entry visa into the States – they can't believe it. They have it photocopied and keep fingering it suspiciously. I handed over my letter from the Palace and asked if I would have to have this letter for life. The officer said yes, but he wasn't sure.

New York – JFK
The passport control lot were very grouchy today in New York. I sat with a bunch of Indians, Iraqi Chaldeans and odd bods, waiting 'til my passport was cleared. The Chaldean lady

chattered away to the Indian, not in the slightest bit bothered that he did not understand a word; she is going to Detroit. I have been fingerprinted and photographed, eight pictures in all. What could they do with so many of them? It took one and half hours to finish with me – two plane-loads had come and gone. The Chaldean lady missed her connection to Detroit, too. My bag arrived torn and wet.

12 December
This afternoon Edward Said gave a talk at the Columbia Presbyterian Medical School. Q said they had a difficult time advertising it. All the posters would mysteriously vanish as soon as they were put up. Halfway during the lecture the fire alarm went off. Edward remained cool as a cucumber. It seemed intentional. The lecture was about ageing and production in the arts. Do you produce differently when you are older? Are you wiser? Beethoven made wild discordant music at the end of his life.

21 December
We all went and saw Edward and Mariam last night. He had just gone through a new kind of chemotherapy, and we had to sit far away from him as he said he was very radioactive! A friend had just telephoned him and said, finally, the Arabs have an atomic bomb! He is an amazingly brave man. I hope this latest cure is going to work.

22 to 25 December
Sol, Q and I are on our way to Mexico for four days and then Honduras. I am obsessed with the volcano Popocateptl, which is puffing away and erupting. It hasn't done that in a century. I love volcanoes, so I am taking this as a personal welcome. Names are impossible to pronounce in Mexico, but what a place. We have a rented a taxi that stays with us. The driver is named Vicente, like the president. Our days are filled with

touring archaeological sites, churches, museums –the best in the world and art. Everything is on a large scale. A six-kilometre path for processions on feast days of the Virgin Mum of Guadalupe and her miracles. Our Vicente says that's what the Vatican envies – the miracles.

Diego Riviera is a revelation.

26 December–26 January 2001 – Honduras

We are in La Ceiba – tropics and the monsoons. Super-lush greenery; what are sold for an exorbitant price in our world as indoor plants are present in the wild here. I saw a tree with great yellow flowers on short stems just growing out of the trunk all the way up, and lots of new birds.

Kiko and Sowf live in a little concrete square house. They keep getting robbed. He's doing his doctorate on the rainforest. We spend the New Year in Esperanza. At the Hotel Esperanza, an Xmas tree at the entrance desk rings the tune of 'Jingle Bells' any time one passes by. We try to phone Ma from the telephone exchange; the guy said, 'Oh, where Saddam is?' Needless to say we could not connect, but we certainly made his day.

Butterflies are so prolific here, big and so bright they give the feeling of flowers in the air.

Back in La Ceiba they are robbed again, so we move to another house.

Honduras has two American fruit companies. They used to be called Standard and United, now they are called Dole and Chiquita. They thought the names more in keeping with the 20th century.

14 February – Beirut

It is like a refrain: Iraq is being bombed again. Thirty-four British and US planes hit five different areas in Iraq because Bush says Iraq poses a big threat to their airplanes. Never mind that they are in Iraqi airspace, and that the no-fly zones are not a UN order. But where are we getting all this new stuff from, considering everything is monitored?

And they call it routine. Since when can you call bombing a country routine? I've switched to watching Iraqi TV, but they don't say anything. In fact, someone is handing out presents to the Palestinians. Poor Palestine. Now that Sharon is in, that's the end of Palestine; it's going to be kill, kill and kill.

18 February

We have been through two US presidents and now the third. Don't they have any imagination? Can't they find another target?

Powell calls Iraq ' the continual threat', and Bush calls it 'Swiss cheese'. I wish the Swiss would sue him. They are building up Saddam again with their propaganda.

5 March

What horrors are going on in the world now:

Animal holocaust in Britain for CJD.

A Palestinian Holocaust.

The UN embargo on Iraq.

Statues of Buddha blown up in Afghanistan.

African holocaust with AIDS … and so on and so on.

Here in Lebanon no one wants to eat Iraqi truffles because they say they are radioactive from the depleted uranium left over from the Gulf War. In fact, they mostly come from the Tikrit area, which suffered less pollution than the south.

David Hirst came for dinner the other night. He is just back from Bahrain, and said Bahrain had become 'the whorehouse of the Saudis', and that he is going to write an article about it. I said, 'Another country you are going to be *persona non grata* in.'

'Saudi,' he says, 'not Bahrain.'

19 March

Am having an e-mail correspondence with Kiko about leaf-cutter ants – they fascinated me in Honduras, lines of neatly cut, same-size bits of green leaf walking in a line. He said that they had attacked his pink *pui* trees on the site, too, but they don't like it too much because it's toxic. I asked how they could eat it if it's toxic.

'They don't eat it,' he said, 'they just take it down their tunnels and chew it; it ferments and grows something they live on.'

So they are really farmers and cultivators. I said that if it ferments, it must be alcoholic, and they might be quite high as they walk in line, bum to bum.

At Khala Munira's today two ladies were talking about the fashion of the *hajj* now. On their return, their cars are covered with flowers and balloons, and at home they hand out chocolates with *sibha* (worry beads) attached and little pitcher in cut glass for *zam zam* water. On leaving, one is given a little bag of goodies like in a kiddies' party, with memorabilia from the holy land.

30–31 March

A Conference on Memory for the Future.

Many Lebanese live in fear of the memory of their past, the sixteen-year civil war. Some statistics from the war: 184,000 wounded; 27,000 missing and lost; 13,400 handicapped; 120,000 dead; 2,000 women killed after being raped and 2,641 booby – trapped cars.

The conclusion of the seminar was that it takes time to judge one's compatriots for the crimes they have committed during any war. That's why we see it's so difficult for most Serbs to let Milosevic go to The Hague, and the Israelis for Sharon re: the Sabra and Shatila massacres. It is only ten years after the civil war has ended in Lebanon that films and books are starting to appear on the subject.

17 April
Ma's latest theory: Iraq's soil is blessed because 47 prophets of all religions are buried there. So it will always be fought over and protected!

29 April
Samir said he was having trouble sleeping, so Ma says, 'I've found the best way. Think of a film you like and follow the story.'

Sol says, 'How about *Gone With The Wind*; four hours later you're still awake.'

'No,' Ma says, 'a simple one.'

A doctor told Q that the best way was to concentrate on your big toe. It's so boring, you pass out immediately.

15 June
Lunch at home: Samir, Minni, Eid, Ma and me. The conversation was about boys and girls playing as kids. My story was about my cousins' daughter May, who was always longing to play with her boy cousins. One day she was found lying on the grass while the boys were jumping and screaming about; when asked why she was not playing with them, she said she was playing dead. Then Ma said when we were young in Delhi a whole troop of friends had come to play with us in the garden. Daddy came out and saw Dood sitting by himself, and asked why he wasn't playing with us; he answered that he was, but he was the daddy. So Daddy hooted with laughter and went in to tell Ma that now he knew where his place was in the household. Minni said her story was worse; playing with her brother Micki, he'd tell her she was the mum and he was the maid, and he'd take the doll and dress and undress her while she would just sit and watch.

12 September
Yesterday, came back about 3 p.m. and switched on the radio as always – the first thing I do when I come in, in case I miss some earth-shaking bit of news. I heard that a plane had crashed into the World Trade Center in New York, so I went to tell Ma that to switch the TV channels.

She was watching *The Hound of the Baskervilles*, a Sherlock Holmes mystery she's seen dozens of times. Regardless – she was glued. I kept going back with more details: 'There's another plane,' I said: nothing doing. Finally the movie was over and we switched to CNN. Well, the USA cannot be the same anymore, and like the rest of the world, we were stuck to the TV. Who could carry out such a synchronized bit of planning? Ma said only Usama Bin Laden is intelligent enough and has the money, which you'd certainly need for an operation like this. Dunia said it could be domestic, like Oklahoma. Anyway, they are not accusing anyone just yet. This is scary: the big and mighty USA is vulnerable too.

15 September
They know the names of the hijackers now, and they are all Arabs. God help us. The USA is preparing for war, but against whom? Iraq, I guess; it's always an easy target, and what is left of poor Afghanistan to bomb? Only Sharon is the winner; he will do what he wants to now.

I am supposed to be going to Greece to take T. A. her painting. What a time to travel with a 2-metre-plus roll of canvas that is packed and looks like a lethal weapon.

17 September – Greece
Well, managed OK at the various airports, but was not allowed to carry it on myself. The staff asked what it was and I told them, 'A painting.'

'So big?' they asked. But it went through the X-ray machine without a problem. T. A. loves the painting. It tells the history of Monemvasia, which is where she has her house.

Two weeks later
I am in Serifos with Panos; we are on the balcony watching the falcons circling overhead and talking to each other. This morning a falcon was chasing a pigeon, and then a whole bunch of pigeons ganged up and chased him away: safety in numbers. Like Bush, I told Panos. He wants the whole world with him to attack Afghanistan, like the whole world ganged up against Iraq. How come the whole world doesn't gang up against Israel?

In Serifos the frogs are large and mute. You see them lurking on stairs, beautiful, fat and silent. I am surprised the scientists haven't used their genes to make other frogs croak less.

4 October
Went to see Avra and Michael, old friends from Baghdad. Michael has been given 70 untranslated Greek letters to Lord Byron to translate. Six of them are from two boyos in love with Byron, but mostly they ask for money or quinine for medicine. Such fun; Avra has written three books and Michael one or two. Amazing. Both are in their 80s, an example to us all.

7 October
On the plane going back to Beirut. Whenever I was going back to Baghdad, there was always this feeling, a slight dread and fear of the unknown. But not so for Beirut: a happy feeling to be going back home.

19 October
The bombing is continuous in Afghanistan. Today's paper says friendly troops have landed, whatever that might mean, in American war lingo.

The anthrax story continues in the USA and now it has been also discovered in South America and Kenya. Butler, in the *Herald Tribune* says it's most probably Iraq. He will never forgive being ousted from there, losing that profitable job. Meanwhile Scott Ritter says it's anthrax made in the USA. Maureen Dowd, that wonderfully witty lady, says Bin Laden might get his wishes fulfilled, for women to be covered. She is now typing with long gloves on and everyone is out buying a gas mask. Not quite the standard gear for cover-up, but it will do.

Cess sent me an e-mail joke yesterday: someone whispers in Bush's ear, 'Your wife is pregnant.'

He answers, 'Must be Bin Laden.'

1 November

In the USA, how you look is what counts now. There have been many incidents of attacks on would-be Arabs; even a poor Indian Sikh was killed because he wore a turban, by someone who thinks Arabs look like characters from the old-time movies, when they roamed around in turbans like in *The Thief of Baghdad*. Wonderful cartoon in the *Herald Tribune* today: Bush at the centre surrounded by his generals, with a caption that says, 'The Taliban's spirits have improved since they have been eating our food drops.'

Does the bombing of Afghanistan to smithereens make any sense?

9 December

Went to Sidon and Tyre today, had lunch on the seafront in the port; the fishermen were mending their nets. All of them, sitting in their boats were using their toes to hold on to strings or bits of net while mending them. I thought what a waste, one doesn't use one's toes anymore. I am going to start using them for brushes waiting to be used while painting. In our childhood we climbed trees a lot but now there are fewer trees and climbing is out of fashion for kids. We might outgrow the use of our toes in years to come.

9 *January 2002*

For a semi-exiled Iraqi, losing a residence permit is not the best situation to be in, but I guess life could be worse. I spent yesterday being interrogated with a lot of minor criminals – passport forgers, thieving or runaway maids, etc. I promised the interrogator a painting and he promised me my permit. But of course it's thanks to Nidal, my magic open sesame, who has come to my aid yet again. I am supposed to be the manager for their poetry reading festival in Bahrain in a few days. Some manager, losing her identity card.

Sol left me a note yesterday before leaving for Yemen: 'Get organized.' Magda has given me an organizer. I told her I doubt I would ever open it. People are always giving me files, hoping that I might put a few bits of paper in them. I am genetically disorganized like Ma. Sol is very neat like our father; Dood is only neat in his architectural work.

17 *January – Pakistan*

It's becoming a yearly habit, to be in Pakistan to see Handy. For me the Subcontinent, India and Pak, are like home, as I grew up in India. People tell me, 'Are you crazy, how come you're going to Pak?'

I say, 'Where do you think you are living, seeing that our whole area is in turmoil?'

Handy is now on the committee for The Kashmir Peace Plan between India and Pak, and has to keep rushing off to Islamabad for meetings.

My bird-watching! Here in Karachi, it's the crows, they talk and talk – they are supposed to be harbingers of news, and some people know how to understand them: naturally, only the old folks anymore.

Meanwhile the Bush-and-pretzel episode continues – it's really very funny, but I can't think why the White House let such an idiotic thing be known, even though it actually happened.

29 January

On the 27th we had a party, and Ardeshar asked me whether I would like to see some paintings. 'Sure,' I said. So at about midnight he takes me by the hand, much to the surprise of all left behind, and we go to his house. We are greeted by four dogs barking away. There I find the most beautiful drawings: prints of portraits of Salvador Dalì's, portraits by Picasso, Manets of his mistress, Rodins, Dalì sculptures and more Picasso. I am in a state of shock and awe at this most exquisite collection. Who says small is not beautiful!

We have a Iranian lady fortune-teller telling our fortunes. Davies is doing her exercise, marching on the grass; I keep telling her not to walk in straight line so as not to make a path in the grass, but it's of no use. Vivaldi is playing on the music machine, and Halim is behind his pillar.

Meanwhile, at the airport, the FBI is checking PIA passengers going to the *hajj* in case of an al-Qaeda escapee. Pakistan is cross because, they say, why aren't *they* doing the checking? Is the US here to stay? Are they slowly easing themselves out of Saudi Arabia? When they have flattened Afghanistan into a desert, it will be easier to put in a gas pipeline from the Caspian, through Pakistan into the Indian Ocean. Easy access.

30 January

We are in Larkhana, Sind, Handy's hometown. A Bin Laden-type figure lights the fire. It seems to be his duty, as he comes in to check it every half hour. At lunch we had river-fish pilau; it's the dish of Larkhana.

I ask Masoud, Handy's brother who looks after their estate, 'Who came to complain today?'

He says, 'A bunch of chaps, relatives of a murderer who had killed a fisherman.'

The real murderer had been killed by a snake, so they brought a relative and Masoud said the verdict was to set him free, but they would have to pay five million *rupee*s to the fisherman's family. The relative of the murderer will come tomorrow hidden in a car, a patrol car ahead of them to clear the way. Once they leave the Khurho house they will be under the protection of the Khurhos and will not be killed. Also, a wrong *mullah* was arrested today, so he was trying to get his name scratched out of the files – lovely lot of tribal mafia dealings.

We go to hear ragas being sung in a *mazar* near Hyderabad: Shah Abdul Latif, Sindi Sufi poet of the 17th century. In the mosque, people are milling about; there are quilts on the floor on which whole families sleep. People use the place like hotel. Ladies very high on the Sufi music are swinging their hair about. Iskandar, the guide accompanying us, says the same ladies come every week. They pretend they have a *jinn* so they are left alone by their husbands. It scares them to have a *jinn*-inhabited wife. The extremes some wives have to go to, to escape ...

4 February

Done it again, at the airport, this time. I left my carry-on bag at the house, so am waiting for Halim to bring it. It's good we came early. The families Afghan fighters – who are called 'friendly fighters' by the USA – get an apology and 1,000 dollars when a soldier is killed by 'friendly fire'. 'Friendly' is a much-used word in this war in Afghanistan.

Iraq, meanwhile has not been let off the hook. They have tried very hard to find a connection between Iraq and al-Qaeda, but with no success. But every now and then they bomb Iraq just to keep it in line, and also as a reserve for when they next need to bomb for some political pretext or other.

28 March – Beirut

The Arab Summit is meeting in Beirut. The first day was an absolute disaster: the Palestinians walked out. The second day, exactly the opposite happened. Abdullah of Saudi Arabia and Izzat Ibrahim of Iraq kissed and looked happy, Iraq and Kuwait shook hands and all the Arabs signed the Saudi peace plan. Let us see how far it will go; now that the Arabs have signed, will Israel accept it?

Amer Musa (head of the Arab League) is clever, witty and charismatic. When Sharon let it be known that he might like to attend the summit, Musa's reply was 'We'll have to see if we can allow him to return to Israel.' That is what Sharon threatens Arafat with all the time.

The Arab world certainly lacks female representation. The conference was a sea of men in suits and *abbayas*. I don't mean that women are the answer, but as we consist of half the world surely we should be working together.

30 March

Blair has gone to see Bush because they are going to join up for an attack on Iraq. Bin Laden has not been found, so it's back to Iraq again: the Weapons of Mass Destruction Syndrome – it's all such a sham one wants to cry, but where does crying get one?

Rafsanjani calls Bush 'a dinosaur with the brains of a sparrow'.

12 April – Amman

Powell has gone to see Sharon, the situation is very sad and there doesn't seem to be any solution. Thousands of Palestinians are homeless, 4,000 arrested, an unknown number killed. Israel will not let any journalists in to see what has happened in Jenin.

The Arabs are, as usual, silent. Europe is sort of trying to help. Will they be able to mount a boycott against Israel?

Ever since Bush's statement ('you are with us or against us'), everyone has their own view of who is their terrorist and acts accordingly. For Sharon, all Palestinians are terrorists, for Russia, all Chechens and so on. Human rights have disappeared into thin air.

Meanwhile, I am in Amman trying to work for an exhibition at the end of this month, I want to cancel it as it is so difficult to work in this terrible situation, but no one will let me. Life has to go on, they say.

25 April

There is nothing to write about except horror stories, so I haven't been writing. But I heard the other day that Rehavan Zaavi, the Israeli tourism minister who was killed and who sparked this whole new fighting, was called 'Gandhi' in Israel not for his views but for his shaven head. He said, 'There is no place for two people in our country … Palestinians are like lice; you have to take them out like lice.' No wonder he was killed.

13 May

Long story to write about re: my exit from Jordan. But first, just to mention that despite everything the exhibition came off very successfully. They said I cheered them up, so there was a purpose.

I came by car to Amman, so I left by car for Lebanon. I arrived at the border; the officer asked, 'Where is your letter from the palace?'

Oh, oh! 'What do you mean,' I said, 'I gave up my residence permit in Jordan one and a half years ago. It's all stamped legally in my passport.'

'Sorry, you can't leave.' This even though I had registered with the police in Amman. 'Anyway,' he said, 'your passport has expired.'

'It has not,' I said, 'I have 'til 2004.'

He said, 'Two weeks ago the Iraqi embassy sent out a memo. You need a new passport.'

I was sent back to Amman.

Next day, I go with Yak to the embassy; it always helps to know someone who knows someone.

'Yes,' they say, 'you have to change your passport, we advertised two weeks ago.'

I said, 'My nephew is in Honduras, he's hardly likely to have read the papers there ... Anyway, can I have a new passport now?'

'No,' he says, 'we don't have them yet.'

'That's lovely, so how am I supposed to leave?'

'We'll give you a safe passage permit, you can get your new passport from Beirut when you get there.'

So I get my first piece of paper.

Then I go to the Jordanian police. Their computer is busted. 'Come back in an hour,' they say. Later, an officer tells me:

'There is nothing in your name here. It is all wiped out.'

So why did they send me back from the border? It could have been the secret police, we think.

We go get a fixer. 'Nothing doing,' he says, 'if it was the secret police you would have been picked up at the border.'

So I am armed with a photocopy of my not being a runaway Filipina, with the telephone number of the police, incase of a problem.

I leave three days later, my heart in my mouth, with two bits of paper as my only protection. At the border I get taken into the inner sanctuary yet again.

'We can't accept a photocopy,' the officer tells me.

So I say, 'You are to telephone this number.'

He makes them read the whole letter over the telephone and then reluctantly stamps my passport. His parting words:

'Better keep this paper with you always.'

'Forever,' I say.

But they didn't ask me for the Iraqi embassy paper, not at the Jordanian or Syrian or Lebanese borders.

Beirut

The new passports have not arrived in Beirut either. 'In a month,' they say, 'maybe.'

A Cess story, to be taken as always with a pinch of salt: He has a friend living in the USA for twenty years, who decided he wanted to marry an Iraqi girl. So he goes off to Baghdad, where they line up 120 girls for him to choose from! I ask,'How did he find so many?'

'He has a lot of relatives,' Cess said. Anyway he chooses this 16-year-old girl and goes back to the States. They have a kid. Now, Cess says, he has gone back to look for another wife! What happened to the first?

'Oh! He divorced her, she had too demanding a mother.'

I said, 'Well, he didn't marry the mother.'

'Well,' he said, 'she kept pestering him to get her a green card and carry money for her, etc.'

So now he has gone back to look for another wife to look after his kid. The poor first wife is back with her mother with no husband and no kid. They saw twenty girls only this time and he liked one, a college girl, but she hasn't finished college yet.

5–6 July

At the Baalbek Festival, the Alban Berg Quartet played in the Temple of Bacchus. It's an open-air concert in the ruins. The Mozart was accompanied by the persistent screech of a baby owl or owls. The Bartòk had bats squealing throughout the concert, and a bat kept dive-bombing the audience, which was the dumbest ever and clapped after each movement. People kept trooping in late. The musicians were very unhappy, a pained expression on their faces throughout. I loved the birds, and wondered what Mozart and Bartòk would have thought of the additional sounds.

24 August
Bush has come out with a new statement or decree, re: the enormous forest fires going on in the USA. He has allowed the lumber people to take out the dead wood plus cut large areas, as if there is a fire it won't be such a big one: lovely bit of environmental protection. On the radio the other day, I heard him described as 'as environmentally friendly as an oil slick.' In the 12th century, a new *wali* (governor) was posted to Iraq and complained about the heat. He was told that this heat is what ripens the date palms – so he gave the order to chop down the palm trees.

14–15 September
The Herald Tribune this weekend had an article about an Icelandic conceptual artist, Hlyner Hallsson, invited to have an exhibition by the Chinati Foundation in Marfa, Texas. It consisted of four graffiti-style sentences in English and Spanish:
  'The real axis of evil are Israel–USA and the UK';
  'Ariel Sharon is the top terrorist';
  'George W. Bush is an idiot';
  'Iceland is Banana Republic No. 1.'
It caused such an uproar that they were threatening to close down the institute. He answered that he had read all these things in the newspapers and that everyone in the USA, everyday, says that George W. is an idiot. So he proposed a sequel. In the second and new part of the exhibition, he wrote:
  'The axis of evil is North Korea, Iraq and Iran;'
  'Osama Bin Laden is the top terrorist;'
  'George W. Bush is a good leader;'
  'Iceland is not a banana republic.'
He added, 'I just wrote now what people want to read.'

21 October

Saddam has just freed everyone in prison in Iraq, except spies for Israel and the USA. Pictures were in the papers today of hundreds rushing out of the prisons waving jubilantly. Saddam says he did it in gratitude for getting a 100% vote to reinstate him for another seven years as president.

Meanwhile, North Korea has now admitted to developing its nuclear capabilities. But the USA wants to deal with them through dialogue. Condaleezza Rice says the difference is that North Korea has no money and might listen (they haven't so far), and Iraq has a lot of oil ... or is it that North Korea has nuclear power and Iraq doesn't? It is well-known that Iraq's nuclear facility was bombed in the 80s by Israel, and even the International Atomic Agency has cleared us. It's safer to bomb Iraq: less dangerous, fewer body bags come home.

24 October

First spontaneous demonstration took place in Baghdad. It seems about 1,600 prisoners are missing of those freed from prison, and their families were demanding to know their whereabouts.

27 October

Went to the Iraqi Embassy to get a new passport; I had been using the old one all this time. It was full of chaps. It turns out that Saddam also declared an amnesty for all army deserters at the same time he freed all prisoners, so everyone wants to return now.

Lots of activity and reporters taking notes – there was good feeling but it was also sad, because they were mostly young men who had run away from military service. They looked much the worse for wear, as if times had not dealt them good cards, or they would already have had a life by now, a future. They are given a white *laissez-passer* to return.

30 October
Magdalena sent me an e-mail. She has found me a publisher and I might be published in Spanish, but I will have to do an update.

13 November
As I update for the new Spanish edition, I look through my notebooks and read about Q's Missoni jacket; I e-mailed to ask about its whereabouts, and I just got an answer. He says he has lost a lot of weight, and so he has it on right now; Sol is arriving, and she will be absolutely livid.

I also notice there is so much missing or lost, because I write e-mails mostly now and not in my notebooks. Jasmina promises one day to publish our correspondence. She, being a writer, keeps her e-mails.

Today the Iraqi parliament unanimously voted against the UN resolution re: letting in the international arms inspectors again but leaving the final answer for Saddam.

14 November
Saddam accepts unequivocally, and Bush is very upset. He is really angry and keeps repeating the same thing. It sounds to me as if whether Iraq has or hasn't got weapons of mass destruction, the USA will bomb. We have been given a month and a half, maybe, for the inspectors to check Iraq out. The USA seems very impatient, and I hope they won't find this wait too difficult.

Ma goes back to Baghdad on Monday, same as the inspectors. I leave on Sunday for Pakistan.

15 November
The Iraqi opposition in the West was supposed to meet today in Brussels, but cancelled it due to infighting about who should be the leader. They also didn't all get visas.

Egypt has three new kinds of dates. They marketed them as Arafat, Saddam and Sharon. Arafat and Saddam sold out; Sharon was not so lucky.

17 November – Pakistan

Back in Pakistan, second time this year. I have an exhibition in February, so I have come ahead of time to do some work.

Handy is in the provincial senate this time. She said every election they work so hard electioneering and don't get in. This time they decided to fill out forms and stay at home ,and she got in. So every morning there are a few chaps waiting to talk to her on the veranda. She is aiming to be Governor of Sind, so she can invite her favourite Indian film star, Shah Rukh Khan, to come over. His picture is all over her computer screen. Handy is helping me out on the computer – she is a whiz at it. As we finish typing sections, they go by e-mail to Sol, always my editor. I wish we could have more of this kind of US technology as opposed to all the war machinery.

The best thing that Musharraf has done for Pakistan is to have 150 women representatives in the National Assembly – some of them veiled, others not – facing the bearded lot, all in one hall with equal rights.

22 November

Met an Afghani lady today, Aisha Gailani. She has just come back from her first visit to Afghanistan in twenty-four years. They rented a house, as theirs had been occupied long ago by various sections of the army. She says it's a tragedy: no water, electricity maybe for two hours a day. No roads, no jobs, people are so poor and no aid filters down to the ordinary Afghan. She says that they all say if any aid reaches Afghanistan it goes to the highly paid UN staff only, and even the local hired Afghans get only a pittance. Everyone is anti-American, and they say, 'Bin Laden was their guy anyway, so why is Afghanistan being bombed?'

27 November

Because of its high ideals, Bush called the USA recently 'the single surviving model of human progress'. Can one consider as progress the new weapons of mass destruction the USA is working on, like the 'People Zapper' (technical name: Vehicle Mounted Active Denial)? The 'Zapper' boils the water in your system to 130 degrees in two seconds, cooking you like in a microwave oven. Their so-called non-lethal weapons include lasers that blind and stun you and cut through metal; well, there is not much left of you if they cut through metal. Then there are gasses like the one used in the Moscow theatre recently, and the electromagnetic or E-bomb.

These weapons are what will be used in Iraq now, this time. They are the latest and need to be tested. Mr Bush and his oil cronies will then have no need to contend with any people, because there will be none, only the oil beneath. If there is any justice in this world, the oil would get microwaved too; experiments can go wrong!

We are three days into the UN inspectors' teams, looking for those weapons of mass destruction, so far so good. But still the USA is not happy, and says it's not the UN but only Iraq that can clear its name. They have to own up to the weapons they have.

So we are guilty no matter what. Being the eternal optimist, I can only pray and hope that war can be avoided.

Postscript, March 2003

6 March 2003—Beirut
With a heavy heart I open my e-mail a number of times a day to read endless opinions for and against the war. But since I received "Is Baghdad the New Hiroshima?" a few days ago I am dazed and haunted.

According to CBS News, my correspondent tells me, the Pentagon's war plan is based upon the "rapid dominance" theory of one Harlan Ullman, formerly "head of extended planning" in the US Navy and, during his tenure at the National War College, a teacher of Secretary of State Colin Powell. Ullman's theory calls for "800 cruise missiles in the first two days of the war . . . one every four minutes, day and night, for 48 hours."

The missiles "will destroy everything that makes life in Baghdad liveable," Ullman told CBS reporter David Martin. "We want them to quit; we want them not to fight. . . . You take the city down. . . . You have this simultaneous effect, rather like the nuclear weapons at Hiroshima—not taking days or weeks, but in minutes."

"Shock and awe," Ullman calls it. Shock there will be. Awe less likely, as so many will be dead by then.

The disgraceful Arabs, who have never learned the meaning of "unity" or "initiative," met in the Egyptian resort of Sharm el-Sheikh last week. All they produced, apart from a slanging match between Libya and Saudi Arabia, was a statement saying no Arab country should help with the war against Iraq. Yet most of them already have US forces stationed on their territory ready for battle. Does that give the US and Britain the right to occupy Iraq, to be the new colonial masters?

The US is waiting for the UN to give it permission to attack, but gives all indications of being ready to do it without permission. The UN, for its part, maintains a shameful silence as Israel invades Palestinian areas, demolishes, kills pregnant women and children and razes houses with people still inside—all this from behind the safety shield of missiles and armed vehicles. This silence is unlikely to change when the US attacks Iraq. The shock-and-awe tactic will mean there are no body bags to send home to America. Iraqi dead will be called "collateral damage" again and quickly forgotten.

Yet North Korea is allowed to go into nuclear production. The gentle North Korean people are to be dialogued with. No double standards here!

I talked to my 85-year-old mother in Baghdad a few days ago. Everyone there is going about his or her normal business, quite used to war tension by now. They seem quite fatalistic.

My neighbour was going to Baghdad and I asked my mother what I could send her. "Nuts, please," she said. So I sent nuts—and chocolates and water purification tabs—and I told her: "In case war starts, please move to my house in the orchard. It's so much safer than yours on the river . . ."

The river is always bombed, because of the bridges. And it acts like a tunnel. It carries so much noise—huge reverberations flow down it.

Another of today's e-mails says that US Marines have confirmed they have already shipped toxic riot control agents, CS gas, pepper spray and calmative gases—like those used in the Moscow theatre episode, when scores of people died? Meanwhile, in Iraq, the UN is dismantling and blowing up all Iraq's weapons. No double standards here!

The world is crying "no to war" but Mr. Bush and Mr. Blair are single-minded and the B-52 bombers have already started arriving in Britain. I've been under those bombers in Gulf War I. The earth shakes even before they drop their lethal payloads.

The United Arab Emirates have suggested that Saddam step down to avoid war, but it doesn't look as if anything will satisfy the United States now except full control of Iraq. And the US will be there to stay. Like Israel in the occupied territories, it will put down roots. What's the difference between one occupying force and another? The US occupies Iraq to spare the world from terror, having convinced 65 per cent of Americans that al-Qaeda and Iraq are allies; Israel occupies the West Bank and Gaza to spare itself from terror.

As fast as Iraqi missiles are being destroyed, so the US and Britain increase their bombing of the no-fly zones in northern and southern Iraq. Getting rid of Iraqi defences: getting ready for the invasion which I think has already started.

21 March 2003

I am sleeping in the sitting room in front of the television these days. Writing doesn't come easy. I am too uncertain and nervous now, and full of foreboding.

This week was supposed to have been an Iraqi cultural week in Beirut, with an art exhibit, a play and poetry reading. The play was cancelled after the first day because war seemed too imminent and the players wanted to get back to their families in Iraq. The poets too.

So only the art remains. I have my sculpture: dozens of figures of all heights painted and standing in line and made from recycled wood collected from a building site. They look as if they are demonstrating. They represent the Iraqi people and I am calling them "We, the people". My German friend Cristina is staying with me and she suggested that. She said that's what they said at the Berlin Wall when they brought it down.

Hopefully we will recycle ourselves and survive.

On the night of the opening, a few days ago, I willed a sand-storm of biblical proportions, for forty days and forty nights. Everyone laughed. I said that would be the only thing that could save us. We have had a huge storm raging in Beirut—and so have they.

I telephoned Baghdad this morning. The US has been kind to us this time and left us with communications and electricity. The telephone rang and rang and finally Ma answered.

"Did I wake you?"

"No," she said. "I was in the garden doing my exercises." We laughed and laughed.

"Did you sleep?"

"Oh yes," she said.

"What is everyone feeling?"

"We are all resigned to whatever our fate might be." Lamia went and had a pedicure and manicure and did her hair. She said if she was going to die she wanted to be neat. Today they will go and check Amal's shop. It's bound to have damage. The ministry of planning across the river was hit. It's 11 a.m. and I feel sick to my stomach. They say the US forces are 150 kilometres into Iraq. What's the difference between Iraq invading and occupying Kuwait in 1990 and America invading and occupying Iraq in 2003? The most powerful nation in the world with the latest weapons of mass destruction is attacking a small country that has been pre-emptively stripped of its defences. Neither country had a UN resolution legalising its attack. Will the UN be able to place sanctions on the US and its "coalition" now—or does that sound like double standards?

In the name of peace and humanity, thousands have to be killed. In the name of liberation, in the name of democracy, there will be a military occupation. Would someone please tell me where the democracy lies in "Either you are with us or against us"?

The Pentagon says 600 sites were considered most likely to be hiding prohibited weapons, but only 75 were visited by the United Nations' weapons inspectors. Why didn't the Pentagon give the names of the sites to the inspectors? Could it be that they wanted to invade and occupy themselves? Will they now plant evidence where none was found, to make their aggression legal?

In the last twelve years of sanctions, the US and the UK bombed the no-fly zones almost daily. Iraq did not manage to down a single jet or do any injury to any country near or far. How, then, is it such a danger to the world?

The US is using precision cruise missiles that can pick out individuals in their cars from thousands of miles away. Iraqis are told to dig trenches and fight with their swords. Space-age warfare meets pre–World War I tactics. This is the most cowardly war of all—a politicians' war, full of lies.

Hope is in the people of the world, demonstrating, demonstrating and demonstrating against this war. It is they who bring us strength and hope for the future.

I am going to be sleeping in the sitting room in front of the television again tonight. If I can write anything else I will send it. But for now this is all I can feel.